Keys on the Road

20 OCT 2021
UC ALL:

CT, a cat story
Voices from Room 6
Looking Back Looking Beyond
onward

Keys on the Road

a country boy's memories

John – Brotun, MD in Boston

Paul J. O'Brien

Wife: Debra – Atty
Cat + Casey

Keys on the Road
A Country Boy's Memories

Copyright © 2017 by Paul J. O'Brien

All rights reserved. No part of this book may be used or reproduced in any form, electronic or mechanical, including photocopying, recording, or scanning into any information storage and retrieval system, without written permission from the author except in the case of brief quotation embodied in critical articles and reviews.

Permission granted by *The English Record* to print the following poem: "Eastern Point." *The English Record*. 63 (Spring 2013) 31. Print.

A few of the reflections are revisions of articles that originally appeared in *The Daily Gazette*.

Book and Cover Design by Nick Alberti
Printed in the United States of America
The Troy Book Makers • Troy, New York • thetroybookmakers.com

To order additional copies of this title, contact your favorite local bookstore or visit www.tbmbooks.com

ISBN: 978-1-61468-392-6

Contents

Dedication — vii

Foreword — 1

Rain — 5

Rustlers on the South Ridge — 9

"Harold, They Need a Good Switching." — 15

The Intoxicating Scarf — 21

"What's this Rosary Thing?" — 23

Forts and Hideouts — 27

Dogs and Cats — 31

"Who's the Toughest Kid in Town?" — 41

"The Fastest Wheels in Town?" — 45

There Were Always Sports — 49

The Trophy — 59

Cheapskate — 65

"I Think He's Dead" — 69

My First Car — 73

How I Got to Paris on a
Catholic School Teacher's Salary — 77

And Then We Could See — 83

On the Edge: Scotch, Birds,
Cell Phones, and Diners — 87

Roger and JFK — 95

"Something bigger was going on here." — 99

Big Apple — 105

Back to Class — 109

Roots — 113

Untranslatable — 117

The Best-Laid Plans — 129

Good-bye, Lash LaRue — 133

Eastern Point — 137

Raquette Lake — 143

Ending and Beginning — 147

Dedication

To Mom and Dad, Leo, Rose, Colin, and especially my brother John who shared in so many of the adventures of growing up. Without John, life would have been much lonelier and much duller.

To those who shared my journey and helped me to grow as a person: in the early years, childhood friends and neighbors in the village of Raymertown; in the maturing years, my mentors, colleagues at school, friends, and most of all, Deborah, my wife, who helped me to see the way more clearly.

To all those who gave me the opportunity to appreciate our natural world, especially the beauty, mystery, and redemptive power of water.

Special thanks to my support and first reader Deborah for always encouraging me to forge ahead and for listening so patiently. Carolyn Nadeau, my niece, for her astute insights that allowed me to refine and improve the memoir. Rick Pepe, a friend, for his editing and his words of wisdom. Elizabeth Cole, for her careful reading and suggestions. Joe Malinowski, for his help in arranging the photographs for publication and for technical assistance. And to Nick, from the Troy Book Makers, for his guidance and support in producing this book.

When I was about a year old, I managed to climb up and over the playpen that my mother had placed me in outside our home in Haynersville. Once out, I started crawling down the sloped lawn to the main highway. When I reached it, I made my way to the middle of the road and took a seated position. Apparently, I began to wave my hands. Father Vaughan, our parish priest, was the next driver who would appear on Route 7. He was planning to stop at my parents' gas station to get some fuel. Seeing me, he stopped his car along the road, got out, and walked over to pick me up. He carried me up to the house and told my mother who had just come outside, "Anna, you better keep an eye on this boy."

Foreword

After being in the classroom for 47 years, I felt the need to tell my story about what teaching meant to me, and so I wrote *Voices from Room 6*, a memoir of my years teaching at Notre Dame and then at Notre Dame-Bishop Gibbons School. I had come to realize in time something that I always felt intuitively — that a teacher is in essence a reflection of who one is as a person. True, there is a body of knowledge that is vital to any teacher's profession, but all of that material, especially in the deep and expansive world of language and literature, is presented through the lens of a person shaped and nurtured by his own family and by his own community. Forces and influences both seen and unseen play a major role in shaping a person to be a presence and influence in the world he chooses. And if one is fortunate enough, one brings an openness to the worlds of others as he steps forward and sees that the strength of his voice is directly related to the respect he gives the voices of others.

When I think of where I started, I am reminded of the opening of *Star Wars* — "A long time ago in a galaxy far, far away...." For it does seem that my early childhood and formative years were in a world with few connections to the modern world of technology that I live in now. Crank phones that connected you via a local town switchboard to ten or so other families on your line — whenever the phone rang, you knew exactly who was getting a phone call; walking two miles on a country road over streams and past scary bulls to a one-room schoolhouse; sitting around the radio with my parents and brother on a Saturday night listening to "Eliot Ness and the Untouchables";

visiting a country store where you could fill up a bag of penny candy for ten cents. For most of my early life, I lived on a farm outside Troy owned by my grandfather. My father worked his father's farm and also worked full-time for the New York State Highway Department. Then with the double work load starting to take its toll, my parents decided that they needed to move, and so we moved to the village of Raymertown, a small town on the road from Troy to Bennington. My father now worked one job while my mother took care of the four children: Leo, Rosemary, John and me. A number of years separated Leo and Rose from John and me, and in a way my parents, especially my mom, raised two different generations of children.

On the farm, I remember the large, old house — chilly, dark, and mysterious. I remember Grandpa sitting in his rocker by the window in the kitchen and how John and I could get on his nerves. The worst thing I recall that we did was bring four or five snowballs into the kitchen and throw them at him. Even though he was limited and walked with a cane, he tried to whack us with his cane. I remember the oh-so-hot summers, running in the hay fields and knocking over bales that somehow stood upright after coming out of the baling machine. I remember when my brother John and I took the udders of two cows standing next to each other and sprayed each other with milk. I remember bundling up and heading for Midnight Mass in a car that was still cold though my father had gone out early to warm it up. I remember looking across the field at Route 7 and wondering where that road might take me.

In Raymertown, located on Route 7, we had our family home until my father died in 1977. Raymertown: so many memories. Ward's Field, where we played baseball, homers flying up and over Route 7, occasionally a ball smashing into a car; the stream behind the house, where we built swimming pools in the summer; the woods and hills behind the house, where we put our imaginations to work, building forts and hideouts; Baker's Garage, the dartboard and the room with candy and ice cold soda bottles that floated among big chunks of ice in an enormous red cooler; the Shermans and their ghostly son Dewey, maybe a cousin of Boo Radley — their house a victim of Halloween pranks; the one-room school house with swings that made you want to see how far you could leap at full extension; and the long hot summer days sitting on the front steps, dying until an idea popped into our heads like a refreshing rain.

Life on the farm and in the village have been shaping forces as I have traveled my pathway. I saw the world in its small town ways and learned. Eventually I would take Route 7 to Troy and then beyond. To New York, Philadelphia, Ireland, England, Spain and many other wonderful worlds. But always there were those voices and those influences that would bring me back to memories of long ago and remind me of the springs that nurtured me. On the journey, I found that for me — and I think it is true for all of us — there are a few places that help us to put it all in perspective, places that allow us to be and to see more clearly. For me those places have often been associated with water: the life-giving rain of summer storms, the stream behind the house in Raymertown, Lake Luzerne and Camp Tekakwitha, the Atlantic Ocean at Eastern Point Retreat House in Gloucester, MA, St. Moling's Well in Ireland, and Raquette Lake at my wife's family's home in the Adirondacks. Each setting has helped me to crystalize my experiences, to see more clearly the paths I have taken and the forces that shaped me. As I forge ahead on my journey, I continue to look back, in wonder. In "Four Quartets," T. S. Eliot says, "We shall not cease from exploration and the end of all our exploring will be to arrive where we started and know the place for the first time."

Rain

Under the canopy of the family's pontoon boat at Raquette Lake, I sit listening to my wife as she tells me about a book she has just finished, Robertson Davies' *Fifth Business*. Behind her, a light rain falls steadily. It is a locked-in rain, one that my father-in-law calls without fondness a "Raquette Lake Rain," meaning a mountain rain that has gotten stuck, one that will last for days.

For many, rain connotes joylessness, depression, and ruined days. Too much rain can breed in some a stream of pessimism. One example of this vision of rain occurs in Ernest Hemingway's *A Farewell to Arms*, a novel in which rain, pervasive and unceasing, becomes emblematic of despair and death.

A sense of depression is what many vacationers feel when the meteorologist announces the rain front that is imminent. Gone is that day at the beach, that longed-for sightseeing excursion, the backyard barbecue, the roller coaster ride at the Great Escape. "Oh no! It's raining. What are we going to do today?"

On our honeymoon years ago in York Beach, Maine, my wife and I thrived during a week of rain. Our photo album tells the gray, rain-swept, foggy story, but it also foregrounds the story of two people in yellow rain slickers who smiled as individuals and together through the rain at the camera. In one picture at the famous gathering point for family photographers, Nubble Light House, I am giving the peace sign.

Two writers who have shared their love of rain are Frederick Buechner and John Updike. In his memoir, entitled *The Sacred Journey*, Buechner says that of all kinds of weather, he loved rain the best. "I would sit in a deckchair in the rain with a tarpaulin over me, hearing it drum on the canvas sunshade over my head, and loved it for leaving me snug and dry from its drenching, loved umbrellas and the oilskin smell of yellow sou'westers and slickers" (12).

In "A Soft Spring Night in Shillington," John Updike speaks of the "cosmic joy" associated with being "just out" of the rain. When it rained, it was his job to turn wicker furniture on the side porch towards the wall, and "in these porous woven caves I would crouch, happy almost to tears, as the rain drummed on the porch rails and rattled the grape leaves of the arbor and touched my wicker shelter with a mist like the vain assault of an atomic army" (*Self-Consciousness* p.34).

In the margin of both books, I have drawn large stars and written the word, "Yes!" "Yes," for one of those special moments in reading, in this case a moment that tells you quietly that you are not alone.

So many moments both in and "just out" of the rain come back to me: a whipping wind and rain directly into my cousins, my brothers, and me as we trudge along in laughter on a dark ocean beach in Wells, Maine; watching the rhythm of the windshield wipers from the warm back seat of my father's Buick on a family trip into Canada; seeing the stream behind the house growing into a river with the strong spring rains; and the experience that has the strongest hold in my mind — taking shelter in our one-car garage as the sky grew ominously dark with an imminent summer storm.

I don't think anyone in my family was aware of my little ritual. I would take the old army blanket from the glider on our porch and walk behind our house, or if I thought my mother wouldn't see me, through the house and down to the garage. The garage had a sliding door which I would close to about the width of my body — shoulder to shoulder. Then I would place the blanket over my head and around my shoulders and wait. From the kitchen window of the house, I probably looked like an eccentric, little monk.

Keys on the Road

The rains came. And I wrapped the blanket tighter. The harder the rain, the more excited I felt. Sometimes it was hard to even see the house, less than 100 feet away. I was both in the storm and out of the storm. Mist rolled and swirled off the roof, hard rain bounced up from the pavement, and sometimes became pellets of ice. Timelessness encircled me. Only when the rains subsided did I begin to be aware of where I was and that I'd best return, with blanket in hand, to the world of others. For an indefinable period of time, I think I had created what a college friend, borrowing from Hemingway, would tell me we all need, my own version of "a clean, well-lighted place."

Rustlers on the South Ridge

In the early 50's, when my younger brother and I were within shooting distance of adolescence, my parents, particularly my mother, must have concluded that we were mature enough to be left home alone for an afternoon. She and my father would take advantage of this budding maturity and attend meetings of The Third Order of St. Francis (a spiritual community that was based on the life and teachings of St. Francis) in the city of Troy on Sunday afternoons. Counting the drive to Troy and back, they were gone about four hours. For the most part we were exemplary young men, but there was one occasion when I strayed off the path and one in which we both were in the rough for a while.

The first example did not have the serious fallout that the second did, but for me, it was a significant issue. For some time, my father had been giving us haircuts. Now his haircuts held up when we attended the one-room school houses — usually only four or five in my one-row class, but when we started school at Our Lady of Victory in the big city of Troy, observations of how one looked became, at least in my mind, a top priority. One's haircut fit into the category of sartorial acceptance. With my parents gone to Troy, I decided that I could give myself a haircut that would be far superior to my father's cut.

I stood in front of the mirror in my brother's room with a newspaper on the floor — large dresser with a big mirror — and began. I held the electric trimmer in my right hand, leaned my head left, and slid the base of the machine up the right side of my face into my hair, just in front of my ear. Once into the hair, I angled the base of the trimmer up and eased the cutting blade slowly out of my hair. I took a hand-held mirror from the bureau and held it up to see my work. It seemed pretty successful to me, although I had taken off a little more than I intended. I returned the trimmer to my face and repeated the process five more times, once in front of the original and four times in the direction of the back of head. A lot of hair fell to the newspaper. I held the mirror up again — maybe I had taken off a little more than I wanted, but it looked neat. Now to match the left side to the right side. I reversed the position and started, realizing immediately that my left hand didn't seem to have quite as much control as my right. "Ouch!" — I had given myself a nick as I was lifting the trimmer away from the head. I took the mirror — a red mark, but no blood. I might have gone a little bit higher on this side — but I could match that up I was sure. I finished on the left side — hand a little more unsteady and my trim line a little higher, but I figured now I could match up on the other side. My head tipped left again, but as I worked, I had a hard time lining up with the previous pattern. I looked — now I was concerned because the line was so uneven. I tried to make the line where the trimmer exited parallel but it was very difficult. When I stopped, I had taken the cut in two of the strips very high on the right side of my head. Ok, stay calm, I thought. I looked carefully at it using the hand mirror. Ok, I said one more try on the left.

Just as I was finishing the left, John walked in, looked at me, and said, "Geezzz." I turned to look at him. "What do you think?" And I turned my head around. He sighed and said, "Uhhhh, that's pretty rough." I said, "Can you fix it?" He looked again, "You went so high that I don't think I can do much."

I stared at myself in the mirror. "Bad, isn't it?" John was working hard not to smile, and then he uttered the word and accented it, "Very *rough*."

We were outside tossing the football around when Mom and Dad got home. I had a winter hat on — a toboggan — so my secret was safe for the moment. Just before supper, I walked into the kitchen with my hat still on. My mother was at the stove. "Mom, got a little problem." She turned to me, "Yes?" I was trying to put my story together. "Well, while you were away this afternoon — you know how Dad cuts our hair every few weeks." She looked directly at me, "Uh hum."

I sat down at the table, "Well, I thought that maybe I would try to cut my own hair. So I got out Dad's trimmer and tried to cut my own hair."

She stared at me, "Yes?" Well, here it is, and I pulled my hat off. My hair was messed up from the hat, but nothing could hide the disaster on the sides. She walked closer and then stared. "Turn your head a bit," she said. I did, and she said, "Oh dear. This is not good."

"I know, Mom, it was a bad thing to do, and I won't ever try that again, but, Mom, I can't go to school with this head. I can't. It would be awful."

She looked at me and said, "I'm glad you learned a lesson. I should just make you go to school like that, but we may be able to figure something out." I got up and gave her a hug. "Thanks, Mom."

That Monday I went off to school with the toboggan on my head and a note from Mom that said. "Paul suffered a head injury. Please allow him to wear the hat until the injury is healed."

Her note was an example of how she sometimes resolved her "right is right" philosophy. She was old school in that you should know that what you do is wrong or inappropriate, but when weighed against her child's fear of humiliation, she chose to show an understanding heart.

So for the next ten days or so, I wore the hat until the hair started to grow back in. And the next time John and I were due for a haircut, Dad took us down to Art's Barbershop in Center Brunswick. Maybe he thought we were ready for the big time.

The Third Order of St. Francis was about to come to an end

in the lives of my parents, and that closure was directly related to a discovery my mother made about what transpired while she and Dad were learning about the wisdom of St. Francis in Troy on a Sunday afternoon.

"Boss," slapping his hips to mimic the sound of a horse, John runs into the kitchen from the living room, "rustlers have cut a hole in the fence on the South Ridge. We have to get down there in a hurry and stop them!"

On the kitchen table in front of me are two shot glasses nearly filled with my father's whiskey — the bottle right next to them. I point at the glasses, and both John and I grab one and down it. We slam the glasses down on the table, as I say, "Let's go." And then the two of us, hands slapping our sides, ride into the dining room for about ten feet. Then the scenario is reversed.

This time, I ride into the kitchen with a different plot line. I address John, who stands at the table, the shot glasses full. "Deputy, I'm going to need you fast. The Wagner Gang is heading for town, and they got guns — you know big trouble brewing." Now it's John's turn. "Well, let's show them who runs this territory!" And we pick up the shot glasses, gulp the whiskey, slam the glasses down, and race into the living room to the sound of thundering horses.

These scenes from old Westerns may have played two or three Sundays, but on the last Sunday, we ran a little late, and thus the smell of whiskey still lingered in the air. We were in the kitchen after welcoming them home when my mother suddenly had an odd expression on her face.

"Harold," my mother said, "do you smell alcohol?"

"A little bit," my father said.

"Check that bottle you have on the top shelf."

My father kept his whiskey bottles on the top shelf of the cabinet by the door. He pulled down the one that he occasionally tapped into. He held it up and stared at it.

"Well, what do you think?" my mother said, growing impatient.

"Ahhhhh, it looks a little down, a little low."

"And that's lower than you remember the last time you had some."

"Just a little below the line I remember."

My mother looked at the two of us, and she knew the answer before she asked the question. "Have you boys been drinking your father's whiskey?"

"We just sampled a little bit," I said.

"Horrible taste," John added.

"Well," my mother said, "this is not going to happen again. I don't know what inspired this behavior, but it will stop now. Do you both understand?"

We nodded together. "And Harold," she added, "we may need to put your drink somewhere else and lock it up. I don't want the boys touching it again." My father nodded.

That was the last Sunday Dad and Mom went to the Third Order of St. Francis. I know my mother concluded that she shouldn't be down in the city when trouble might be brewing on the ranch.

"Harold, They Need a Good Switching."

If she had her wish, my mother would have become a teacher. Salutatorian of her high school class — her twin brother Lawrence was valedictorian — my mother wanted to go to college. Her mother told her that only one of them could go to college and that would be Lawrence; besides, my mother was needed on the farm, especially since she was the only girl of the six children. My mother had shared with me some of her memories growing up in a piece she called "What it was like in the old days." What came across was both her love of family and her loneliness. With her five brothers upstream swimming in a natural pool — they swam naked — she would be isolated downstream, sometimes sitting on a favorite large rock. What was strong in my mother was her moral and spiritual sense, most likely influenced by her own mother, and she, in turn, shaped our spiritual lives through Church and prayer and example. Her most powerful line to us was "Right is right, and you know what is right." John used to argue a bit with her saying, "Mom, maybe a little grey sometimes." And she would look at him and say, "John, you know what is right." If either of us got feisty or contentious, she had another line, "Don't be bold."

She ran the discipline program in the house. But on a few occasions, she would have my father execute what she wished to have done, a large degree of that due to her losing battle with arthritis. She might, for example, while we were on a family trip and my brother and I were acting up in the car, say, "Harold, slap them." My father would reach around and try to slap us, futile gestures which we could easily avoid by leaning way back in the seat. There was one occasion though in which my mother slapped me, the only time I remember that she ever slapped me.

We called him Gladiola Joe, a flower hustler with a huge ego and a thick head of hair, who was able to dazzle the young boys in our village with the big rewards that were in store for us after we weeded his gladiolas. "How would you kids like to make enough money to go to New York City? How would you like to buy your own suit for Easter next year? Or buy a new baseball glove?" We were dazzled by his carrots. "Stick with me, kids, and you will make a mint."

I remember weeding flowers the first day in his field: except for a lunch break to eat a sandwich my mother had made, it was non-stop weeding. At the end of the day, Joe, looking fresh as a daisy, sauntered up to John and me — he had already dealt with the other kids. "Paul, you did two rows — you know what that means, son? You get two dollars. And John, you did a row and a half — you get dollar and a half." At eleven or twelve, that still seemed like pretty good money, although it had been awfully hard work weeding those rows.

During one week, following a lot of rain, John and I agreed to come back in the early evening and do more weeding until it was nearly dark. For two nights, we were slaves to the work, but on the third night, I said to John shortly after we arrived, "Hey, let's forget weeding tonight and go down to Vlads and play some pool." A relatively new family in our village, the Vlads owned a nice pool table, a rare sighting in our village. John didn't have a strong allegiance to the weeding, and so off we went.

We were in the middle of the fourth or fifth game in Vlad's garage — five or six of us rotating and playing the winner — when I saw my father driving up the back road, my mother as shotgun. Through the garage window, I could see my mother's face — and I knew that face — sober and serious. I grabbed John by the arm and said, "We've got to get home — fast."

With our bikes, it didn't take us long to get home, and I thought we might be safe. We were both upstairs when I saw the car come in the driveway. Within minutes, my mother's voice, "Paul, come down here for a minute."

I started down the stairs, my mother at the bottom looking up at me with a very stern expression. I reached the second step from the bottom.

"Where were you tonight?" she asked.

"Up weeding in the flower field."

"No, you weren't," she said.

"How do you know?" I said boldly.

"Because your father and I felt sorry for you two," I could feel the intensity building, "and so we made some Kool-Aid and brought it up to you, but you weren't there. You were NOT there."

I was silent, probably shuffling my feet a bit.

"So you go up to your room and stay there — I don't want to see you down by the television. And don't pull such a stunt again."

As I turned, I moved up to the next step and mumbled something like "Yeah, sure."

My mother said, "Come back here."

I walked down two steps, one above her, and she slapped me, the first time she had ever slapped me. "And don't mumble!" she said.

Although my brother John was intelligent and blessed with a quick wit and a great sense of humor, he sometimes let his brain slide out of the frame. Hiding a *Playboy* underneath his socks in the top drawer of his bureau when my mother laundered and put fresh socks away was not a wise move. All I remember about the discovery were my mother's words to John, something like, "Tonight, you, your father, and I will discuss your having this magazine in our house." The problem with hearing something like that was the timing: rather than get it over with quickly, you had the rest of the day to experience growing apprehension. Not that it didn't also give you the chance to build your case for why one should have Hugh Hefner's world under one's socks.

I stood in the living room looking into the framed glass of the picture of my brother as a newly ordained Catholic priest. Behind the glass was my brother Leo, the priest; in the reflection were my brother John, my mother, who was questioning him about the *Playboy*, and my father to her left.

"Okay," my mother said with her ring of authority, "why do you have this magazine in our house?" From where I was, it appeared that the magazine was on the table, facedown I am sure.

To my amazement and disbelief, John said,"Uh, it has some pretty good articles I wanted to check out. There's that baseball article — did you have a chance to look at it?"

I nearly gagged. My mother stared at John and then began, "Now look, there is no room in our house for such stuff as this magazine. John, you should know better than to bring this home. I am very disappointed in your judgment, young man...." As she went on, my brother and my father stared at a wall and a refrigerator respectively. Suddenly, she reached for the magazine, twisted it with her two hands, as if she was wringing the *Playboy's* neck, and then turned to my father thrusting the thing in his direction, "Harold, burn this!"

As chairs began to squeak, I stepped back from my viewing screen and withdrew into the living room. John walked in and gave me a combination grimace and half smile, as if to say, "Whew, that's over — but not that bad."

Two weeks later, I was looking for a hammer, and I went down to the barn where my father kept his tools. Reaching his workbench, I looked over to the far left and there sat John's *Playboy*. The fire had not consumed it.

Summer was just getting underway in our little village of Raymertown. It would be another long hot summer, made somewhat more tolerable by whatever our cool creative minds could come up with. There were the practical inventions, like damming up the stream behind the house using sod and burlap bags to create our own swimming holes, or my brother and me trying to build a raft and head upstream to find what mysteries lay there — except the raft kept drawing serious leaks — or building forts in the woods, where we could hang out as members of a bird gang. And there were the temptations: a pack of L&M Cigarettes purloined by Rich from his mother's carton; loose change that my older brother kept on his bureau — would he see the missing quarter that would allow me to buy three candy bars and two sodas; or the Barry barn, up the road a bit, the barn that my mother had warned us about: "Stay away from that barn; it's too dangerous."

I stood on a beam about 10 feet above the hay, but a heavy wide beam, so I didn't see danger. The game was freeze, and I was "it." I had frozen John and Rich, but had Jean and Dale left. Jean was on the floor, peeking out from a stall, in a green t-shirt and cut off shorts, and with short blond hair and her beguiling smile, she was the cat's meow. If I ran across the beam, jumped to the hay on the next landing, where she couldn't see me, I might have a shot of slipping up near her. Looking back, I saw John and Rich frozen — and no sign of Dale. Jean was the goal. I mean, wasn't she the real object of everyone's desire in the game of freeze, to be frozen by her or to freeze her?

Leaping on a loose pile of hay on the lower landing, I turned and saw in the open doorway of the barn the hood of my father's car. I leaned to my left and saw my mother in the driver's seat. "Oh crap," I mumbled.

"John, quick — get down here. We gotta go."

We walked together toward the car, its passenger window open, and heard my mother's words, "Get in the car. I told you two not to come up here. Tonight, your father is going to give you both a switching."

The afternoon was long and lazy, as we awaited my Dad and the switches. Knowing our father, we were not in total fear and trembling — still, my mother's words had power over him. He might kick it up a notch or two for her.

"Harold, take them out to the woodshed and give them a good switching." My father stood in the doorway of the kitchen, green workman's pants and shirt, huge sweat circles under his arms. He radiated weariness from his day's work. At this point in his life, he had been promoted to foreman in his region for the New York State Highway Department. His job, as I grasped it, was to set the workload for each of 4 different road gangs each week and then drive from one gang to another to supervise their work. Sometimes at dinner he would have stories of the men who were in the gangs. He liked most of the men, but the challenging ones he called, "Ginks." On the way home, he usually stopped at Starkzies, a grocery store in Center Brunswick, situated precariously on a steep bank. There he would buy a wedge of extra sharp cheese and a beer and close his work day with a little taste of relief. Hearing an order to "switch them" was the last thing he wanted to do when he got home.

We stood outside the kitchen in a kind of short walkway, my father behind us. "Break off a few branches of that bush near the outhouse," he told us. We rounded the corner and approached the scraggly bush, a few branches with some zip, but many dried up and feeble. We broke off the weakest of the branches, and I took John's and added it to mine.

My father had opened the woodshed door and signaled us inside. The woodshed was our favorite place to gather with our friends — a homemade ping pong table that favored the home team, a dartboard, and a 45 rpm record player, often spinning with Pat Boone, Ricky Nelson, Fats Domino, and Chuck Berry. "Ok," he said, taking the limp branches from me. "I got to whack you a few times each. It won't be bad."

I was first. I had jeans on and when the branches hit me, it felt like someone had run a worn-out broom across my butt — kind of a sweeping motion back and forth as one sweeps light dust. Four or five sweeps and Dad said, "Ok, you're done. John!"

I watched my brother get the "punishment," and when Dad was done, he said, "Now look, when you leave here and go into the house, let your Mom think you got whacked pretty good." I looked at John, we exchanged a quick smile. I opened the sliding door and stepped out, John right behind me. When we passed my mother in the kitchen, she said, "There, did you learn your lesson?" Heads down, we nodded. "We understand, Mom."

The Intoxicating Scarf

As soon as my mother heard that Our Lady of Victory Grade School was opening in the fall, she drove down and registered my brother and me. Until that moment, our education, through fourth grade, was in a one-room school house. For me grades 1-2 in Cooksboro School; grades 3-4 in Raymertown School: both schools with eight grades in a single room. Now for the first time, I would be in a classroom with students in the fifth grade only. It was kind of scary and exciting too. Each year we would have a different teacher, and each class had about as many students as were in eight grades in my one-roomer.

By the fall I had made a number of friends — Sam, Allen, Frank, Tony, Bobby — and then there was Ellen. She was beautiful, and I had an instant crush on her. She was the radiant center of a group of girls, and I was just one of many small stars in her universe. But I was granted a special gift. Heading out for recess one cool November day, I was trailing behind Ellen and a few of her friends. As she sort of twisted through the closing door, her scarf flew off. She didn't see it and kept running. I looked around and no one was there, so I picked it up and held it like an incredible treasure. I looked around again — no one. I quickly folded it neatly and compactly and put it in my coat pocket. And then I went to the playground to join in the fun.

Ellen stood next to Sister Anne. "Class," Sister said, "Ellen can't find her scarf. It's green with some magenta and orange patterns in it. Did anyone see it?" There was some mumbling, some "I don't knows," and then Sister said, "Keep your eyes open." She patted Ellen on the shoulder — "It's Ellen's favorite scarf. Don't worry, dear, it will turn up."

That night I took the scarf to bed with me, holding it close and breathing it in, imagining Ellen running towards me with her incredible smile, the scarf flying in the wind behind her. Each morning I would hide it in the room that was my older brother's, no longer occupied by him.

And then one day about a week later, I decided that I had to act. Ellen was with three of her friends in the lunchroom, and I was at the far end of the table across from my friend Frank. "Hey, El," Tina said, "you ever find your scarf, the one you lost?" Ellen looked up from her sandwich, "No, it's so strange. I remember I had it on to go out — and it's as if it just disappeared. I loved that scarf."

That night was my last night breathing in Ellen through her scarf. The following day, I went back to our classroom a little early from lunch. The door was open, and I entered. No one there. I went to the coat room, reached into my pocket, and pulled out the neatly folded scarf. I shook it a few times to create a more natural look, and then tossed it up on the rack above the coats, towards the back where it wouldn't immediately be seen. I quickly left the room and then popped into the bathroom, to provide cover in case anyone was checking at lunch.

After the last bell as we were getting ready to leave, Abby, a friend of Ellen's, screamed. "Oh my God," she held the scarf, "El, this is it!" Ellen approached and reached out for it — "Wow! — I don't believe it. Where was it?" Abby was wide-eyed, "I just saw a little bit of it hanging over, but I know the color." Ellen held the scarf close, and then wrapped it around her neck.

I followed them out that day, sad to no longer have my talisman, but kind of happy it was back where it belonged.

"What's this Rosary Thing?"

It's dusk in the early fall, and we are in the backyard playing football — three against three. My brother John and I, along with Rich, against Kenny, Dale, and Roy, all kids from the village. Our house is located at the far end of Raymertown, but the action tonight has come to us. In my memory we have the ball, game very close, when we hear my mother's voice. "Paul, ... John, time to come in, time for the Rosary." The action has come to a complete halt, and I say, "Sorry, guys, got to go." Dale, a skinny kid not blessed with athletic skills, says, "What's this Rosary thing?" I say, "Kinda hard to describe quickly — kind of a long prayer. Want to join us?" The others are walking away, but Dale hesitates and then says, "Ahhhh, maybe, I don't know. Like to just see what it's about."

I can't remember how old I was when my mother introduced the Rosary to my brother and me. For us, it was basically an extension of a prayer my mother had given us a long time ago, the "Hail Mary." That prayer was probably the heart of her prayer life, and it was strengthened by a vision she once had as a young girl of the Blessed Virgin Mary. My mother was no saint, but when I stand back it is hard to find serious faults with her. Maybe the most serious might be linked to her Catholicism and the limits it placed on her and her world view. "No, you can't go to that party," she said. And when I asked why, she responded, "Because Linda," the one giving the party, "is Lutheran and most of her friends are Lutheran." And when I pressed further, she said, "I don't want you getting serious with someone who is not Catholic." Over time my mother came to see that such a Catholic perspective on the world had its limitations. Near the end of her life, she was more tolerant, understanding, and accepting than she had ever been. "How do we know what she's going through," my mother might say about an old friend who had grown distant and cold. "We need to be patient and say a prayer for her."

The rosary is a physical string of beads that allows one to keep track of the different parts of the prayer, with the crucifix as the starting point. Often, the rosary that people possess is linked to a very special event or person. I still have, for example, one of my mother's rosaries. The prayer itself honors the Virgin Mary, the Mother of Jesus. It begins, while holding the crucifix, with "In the name of the Father and of the Son and of the Holy Spirit," followed by "The Apostles' Creed," kind of a summary of the Catholic Faith. Then a single bead where one prays the "Our Father," the response Jesus gave when his disciples asked him to teach them how to pray, followed by three beads — a Hail Mary at each. After the three beads, on the string or cord, one says the "Glory Be" prayer, a short prayer praising the Trinity, the three persons of God. In a way all of this has been introduction to the heart of the prayer. The next single bead is where the one leading the prayer announces the first mystery or key event in the lives of Jesus and Mary. (When I was growing up, there were fifteen mysteries: five Joyful, five Sorrowful, five Glorious; the Church later added the five Luminous mysteries.) For example, the leader would say that the first Joyful Mystery is "The Annunciation," the moment when the Angel Gabriel announces to Mary that the Lord is with her. Then the leader, hands on a bead, says the Our Father, and the rest join in. Ten beads follow, and at each one, the Hail Mary is recited. After ten Hail Mary's, one says the "Glory Be to the Father," announces the Second Mystery, says the Our Father, and the process is repeated for the next Four Mysteries. The prayer ends with the "Hail, Holy Queen," a prayer of petition to Mary.

What might seem to be a little complicated became very familiar to John and me, especially because we said it every night. We became locked in and expected the Rosary each night, though we found it annoying when it came at certain times — for example, in the middle of a football game. But over time and when we were young, one develops strategies that help to make a half hour prayer more tolerable. Let me set the scene.

Somewhere in the 9 — 10 p.m. range, my mother would announce that it was time to say the Rosary. Sometimes, her announcement followed the arrival of the dancing girls on the Dean Martin Show, or whatever show had dancing girls. I would usually be the one to turn the sound down — notice turn the "sound" down. Now imagine this scene: my mother, despite her arthritis, kneeling as upright as she could in front of her chair, her back to the TV; my father, kneeling in front of his chair, but collapsed way down in it, resting his head on his forearms; John and me kneeling up or slouched down, depending on the situation. If the dancing girls were on, we knelt up because we looked into a mirror that showed the girls dancing away; if the dancing girls were not on, we took turns slouching. We took turns slouching because we had our "50/50" action — at least that's what we called it. Once we had established who went first, we simply alternated the activity each night. For the first half of the rosary — up to the middle of the third decade or Mystery, one of us would rub the other's back. For the second half of the Rosary, we would simply reverse positions. What made this a bit tricky depended upon when you were handed the rosary. Usually my mother started the Rosary and would pass the beads to me, me to John (if we were rubbing each other's backs, we had to be cool), John to Dad, and then back to Mom. Dad for some reason — and I smile to think about it — could never remember the fourth Sorrowful Mystery — the Carrying of the Cross. Like Rick Perry trying to remember that third branch of government but unlike Rick in that my mother would "save" him in an exasperated tone — *The Carrying of the Cross.*

The Rosary was a permanent part of our lives. I remember numerous times, for example, returning from Brant Lake late Sunday afternoons after visiting my brother who lived there as a seminarian, hearing my mother's voice say, "Time for the Rosary." As night closed in, the only words in the car were the incantations of Mary's prayer. The day before my sister got married, with her as part of it, we said the Rosary together, with everyone in tears. She was leaving for Michigan after the wedding and honeymoon to live with Colin, her husband, who was returning to continue his studies at Michigan State.

As I wrote in *Voices from Room 6,* my mother's end of life came with the "Hail Mary" being said by all of us in the family as we held hands around her hospital bed. The Hail Mary was a prayer that was central to her prayer life, a prayer that she had given to us, and a prayer that we were now giving back to her.

Our football playing friend Dale came to the edge of the living room that night, where I explained the logistics of the Rosary — kneeling, passing the beads, the solo and choral parts, the approximate length of the prayer. He listened attentively and then said, "Hey, you know what, I really gotta run — thanks for the breakdown. Maybe another time." I offered Dale a chance on a couple more occasions, but he never joined us for the Rosary.

Forts and Hideouts

We heard the fire trucks in the distance and assumed that they were responding to a fire somewhere local, but then Rich said, "Oh my God, I see truck lights on the ridge near the Bornt farm." The fire fighters were heading our way, after someone must have called about a reported fire in the woods. To the little stream adjacent to our fort we raced to fill containers with water and returned to douse the fire, which had been a pretty good size blaze from the dry wood we had thrown together. On the few occasions we had camped out, we lit a fire, gathering nearby wood. Fire gave us a sense of safety and a touch of warmth on cold nights, but we had never expected a response from the fire company in Raymertown. The five of us sat motionless — we could now see a truck at the far end of the field, and we could hear voices. "Jesus, I don't see anything." And "You sure she saw a fire in the woods?"

After apparently assuring themselves that there was no sign of a fire, the men got in the truck and headed back down to the village of Raymertown. We had dodged a bullet. In looking back, it seems forts and hideouts brought with them elements of hope and surprise and danger and sometimes near misses.

We had been digging for about two hours inside a little shack we had put up near the back stream. The plan of our bird gang — we called ourselves birds: I was Eagle, my brother was Hawk, Rich was Crow, etc. — was to dig a tunnel from the inside of the shack to the back yard of our home — a distance of about a sixth of a mile. I think it was Hawk's idea — wouldn't it be cool if we could just step outside our house, pop into the tunnel, travel without being seen, and emerge on the inside of our shack?

We had dug a hole about three feet deep and maybe three feet wide — not a lot of room in the shack, so we had to keep taking dirt outside. I remember feeling exhausted and saying something like, "I am not sure this plan is going to work." We convened — the five workers with the two shovels and one hoe. "Well," Hawk said, " Uhhhh, we might have to let this project slide." We looked at the hole and at our hands, now showing the signs of blisters. "At this rate," Crow, who had lit up one of his Mom's L & M's, said, "it would take us about two and a half years." And with that projection of job time to completion, all work stopped. We would just have to walk the land's surface and dream about the tunnel that would have been so cool.

The coolest fort we ever built was under the remains of the old stagecoach bridge. In our day, all that was left of the original bridge were two huge logs that served as the main support beams for the bridge itself. But they were enough for us to build on. Below on the rocks in the stream, we laid boards and nailed them together for a floor. Then we built a three-sided fort with the open end looking downstream — we could actually sit in the cabin and dangle our feet in the water. We laid boards across the two beams to create a roof for our little house, and made a trap door in one corner, with a ladder down into the house. It was the best. Especially on those lazy days when we smoked a few of Rich's mom's L &M's.

Alas, its life was brief. John and I had traveled for a few days with our parents to the shrines in Canada. When we returned home and popped up to see our coolest fort, we were horrified at the destruction — walls knocked in, floor boards ripped up, and even the trap door gone. When you looked downstream, you could see where pieces of wood had gotten caught on branches and along the shore. We suspected it was a gang of kids from another village, but we never found out for sure. All we had left were our memories of looking downstream through cigarette smoke, our feet dangling in the water.

The most creative place in our world was Bornt's hay barn, located literally a stone's throw from our house. I used to take stones and throw them on the tin roof, watching them as they skipped up and over the roof and down the far side and then sometimes slide back down and off our side. It was more fun than skipping stones on water. Inside the barn were bales of hay, and it was among these bales that we probably had the most fun during the long summers. We built tunnels that would have impressed engineers, long straight tunnels that could descend on half-bales of stairs or rise in stairs to attic-like spaces. There were hideouts in the hay — small spaces which had a bale in front of them — where one could take a breather and plan a strategy of how to escape getting frozen or jump out to freeze someone. We also had a lookout tunnel along the inside wall that faced the road leading up to the barn. Each one of us was supposed to check the road during the games. One day we were so caught up in the game we didn't see or hear the Bornts until it was too late.

We heard the doors open and Ray Bornt yell out, "Ok, back it up right to here." We were all separated, but if my feeling was a measure, we were all scared out of our minds. Frozen. Then the work started as the Bornts — I think four of them — began to unload two large wagons of hay. At one point, I heard Ray yell out, "Jesus, these Goddam kids have been in here again. Looks like part of a tunnel. I told their folks to make sure they stayed the hell out of here. Goddam kids."

Would they find us? The bales kept coming in. Would we be able to get out? I could sense the bales above me and prayed like crazy that our tunnels wouldn't collapse — would we be crushed under bales? Should I shout out for help? What would the Bornts do to us? But the bales held, and I heard the tractors start up and the barn doors close. We waited. Silence. Then I called out, "You guys ok?" One by one, voices emerged from deep under the hay, and we slowly and carefully dug our way out. We made a decision that day that we probably should take some time off from the barn, even though it was great fun.

* Years later I drove past my old home, and the barn had been razed. Gone now as a physical building, I thought of how real those days still are to me. In the barn, I can taste the dryness in my mouth, my fingers burn behind the tight binding string as I move a bale into position, and the barn's tin roof jangles in the wind. As I sit on a bale, I am intoxicated by the sweet aroma of the hay, and gazing about, I see once again the summer world we have created.

Dogs and Cats

There was always a dog around when we were growing up. On the farm, I remember the family that lived in the other part of our house had a German Shepherd. And maybe because the Shepherd was a good dog, my father, once we had moved to the village of Raymertown, made dogs a part of our life. With the exception of Bonnie, a Yorkshire Terrier that my mother loved, our dogs stayed outside. I am not sure how they made it through the winters; all they had was their dog house and sometimes the lower barn.

A few of the dogs are still vivid in my mind: three German Shepherds, a Yorkshire Terrier, an Airedale, and a mutt. Rex and King, two of the shepherds, both liked the water, and that affinity was especially meaningful to my brother and me when we were building a swimming pool in the back stream with burlap bags filled with sod. Water snakes would drop from branches or slide off rocks into the water, but if one of the dogs was around, the snake was flirting with big danger. On a few occasions, I would see the dog emerge from the water with a snake in its mouth. He might then drop it for second, get a better grip, and then snap it hard in the air. A few more times, and it was usually over: a short, intense drama that created for us a sense of safety.

Both Rex and King had sudden endings. Our house was situated at one end of the village of Raymertown, and though cars slowed somewhat when they got to the center of town, they were still going at a good speed when they passed our house. Across the highway was some heavy undergrowth and an attractive world for dogs that liked to explore. At night Rex and King were usually tied to a long rope, but in the day they had some freedom around our house, and they naturally would cross the road into the dense undergrowth across the way. Screeching breaks followed by an awful thump and then the animal cry — I recall that both Rex and King met their fate this way.

Gunther was a huge shepherd — he had come from a church rectory in Ramsey, New Jersey. I remember on one occasion that my father let him venture into the house. He looked bigger than our stuffed sofa, and I remember my mother saying, "Harold, you need to take him outside." He could easily have knocked my mother over. Gunther seemed fine until the day he ventured up the road to the neighbor's pond, where fifteen or so of the neighbor's ducks enjoyed their leisure time. I did not see the massacre, but he killed four or five. Needless to say, the neighbor was angry, and it's a good thing he wasn't home that day because he might have shot Gunther. That was the last day for Gunther — my father gave him to a friend.

Bonnie was a Yorkshire Terrier that my mother found to be a good pal. This affection of my Mom's stands out in my mind because my mother never really had any pets; they were much more my father's and were in his world. And when I think sometimes of the long days of my mother, almost all of it in the house, cooking and baking and cleaning for us, I think of how she must have felt loneliness. To see her holding this little dog and smiling and talking to Bonnie was pretty special. And then the dog showed some breathing irregularity and my parents took her to the vet. She was diagnosed as having a slight problem with a heart valve, and the vet suggested minor heart surgery. He told my parents that there was no real danger, but in the surgery, something went wrong and Bonnie's heart failed and she died. I remember being angry and telling my mother that the vet "told us there shouldn't be a problem," but she didn't want to pursue the issue any further. "Time to move on" was her message, but I know that my mother felt the loss. She filled her days with being a mother to us, praying, cooking, and cleaning, but there was a lot of alone time. Bonnie had helped to fill that void.

Captain was an Airedale that my father loved to wrestle with, but he kept him in a more confined, fenced-in area between the house and the woodshed. It was during this period with Captain as part of our lives that my father began to experience some health issues. I think Captain remained with us in the early stages of my father's illness, and he was some relief for my father, who still wrestled a bit with him, but once the illness began to get a grip on my father, we had to let Captain go. He was, after all, pretty much my father's dog.

But the dog we loved the most — I know I did — was Rusty, a mutt of probably three or four different breeds. I think he was the first dog who actually hung out with us, and when we built forts in the woods behind the house, he would be there chasing squirrels or rabbits or any creatures that drifted by. I remember walking to the frog pond on the Bornt farm that was located behind our house. I have a hard time admitting this, but I held the record of frogs killed by a BB gun in one day — I had 21. I recall that Rusty would watch me, watch the frog get hit, and sink into the water, and then Rusty would look at me as if to say, "What are you doing that for?"

My father looked tense, on edge, one Saturday morning as we sat down in the kitchen to have some breakfast. He was leaning against the sink in his green work clothes, and he held a pliers in his right hand. "You boys enjoy your cereal," he said, "and you can fix some toast for yourselves." He fidgeted with the pliers, "and stay in the house for a while." He headed toward the back door, "Just stay in the house."

Once he was out of sight, John and I, not even touching the Wheaties box, headed at full steam through the dining room, then the living room and to the porch, where we exited on the far side of the house. We ran out the door and cut right, down across the back lawn, past the outhouse, and toward the space where we kept garbage cans. We saw Rusty, leaning on a garbage can, head down, horribly swollen. I said, "Rusty, Rusty," and he lifted his head a little, and I saw the quills. So many quills around his face and his mouth. I think we were frozen in place, when my father rounded the corner — apparently he had gone back inside for something else.

"I told you to stay in the house! Now get outta here! Right now!" My father had spoken forcefully once or twice in his life, to my recollection, so this moment was special, urgent. He face was flushed, and he was squeezing the pliers slowly. We stepped back and turned away, afraid for Rusty.

I remember walking slowly with John back to the porch, neither one of us talking. We sat on the front porch, on the glider, slowly rocking. I am not sure how long it was, but we heard my father's pick-up truck start up, and then watched as he slowly drove by the house and out to Route 7, the main highway. We both knew that Rusty was in the truck's bin and that his life was over.

Years later, I was in a writing workshop, and we were asked to write about a vivid moment from our childhood, one that remained a permanent part of our memory. I wrote this poem:

Rusty

"Don't go back
Behind the woodshed,"
My father said.
My brother's bullet glance
Said otherwise.
Flinging the porch door open
We raced across the back lawn
Rounded the outhouse And slammed to a stop.
Rusty was standing
But his head was low
Close to the garbage can
I stepped forward
And whispered "Rusty"

All I could see
As he lifted his head
Were dark needles protruding
From his swollen face.
"I told you not to come out here!"
— My father held in his hand
A pair of pliers —
And we retreated.

A short time later
From the front porch
I watched my father's
Blue and yellow pick-up truck
Heading toward
The state highway.

"If you don't come and pick up this cat immediately, I am going to drown her!" That was the message my father-in-law had given my wife about Sparky, a family cat who had endeared herself to Debbie one long week when the rest of the family was on vacation and the tiny creature would nestle inside Debbie's arms and bat the pencil she was using for her college work. They became buddies, but our marriage had separated the two until this moment.

For some reason, Sparky had not been a hit after Debbie left. Both her father and brother were not cat lovers, and even though her sisters liked the cat, they led busy lives and didn't pay her a lot of attention. So a few exasperating things had added up and thus the ultimatum.

It took Sparky about two weeks to settle in to our fifth floor apartment and to get used to me. And then she had a home for eleven years in the apartment and for four years in our house. She was nearly twenty when she died.

I never really knew cats growing up, maybe seeing an occasional one curled up on a sofa in a relative's home. Living with

Sparky made me aware of the nature of felines: cats are definitely their own creatures, and they respond when they feel like it, not when you expect them to. Sparky had a special link to Debbie — she often would climb up on her when Debbie was relaxing or reading a book. It was good drama watching Sparky reach a point at which she wanted Debbie to stop reading. She would take her paw and physically try to push the book away. If Debbie was about done with her reading, she would give in to Sparky, but if she wanted to read more, it was a test of wills, and Debbie sometimes had to resolve it by wrapping Sparky in the familiar afghan that was always near her. Then I would enjoy the next act as Sparky tried to figure out how to get out of the afghan. Another moment: waiting for Debbie to walk down our long apartment hallway after work with Sparky running down to welcome her was a trip. I had never seen a cat run to greet her owner and then lie down to be rubbed by her owner until Sparky and Debbie performed that feat.

The only time she ever hissed was if strangers tried to pick her up or upon seeing her for the first time immediately tried to pet her — even when we would tell people that they needed to give her room and time. Some people can't resist the "Isn't she cute!" Then they reach down and are shocked by the hiss and sometimes the scratch.

I realized that cats have intuitive power, at least that is what I concluded from my most memorable example. Early in the fall one year, I had blown out my back with a sneeze. The pain was so great that the slightest move pushed the razor-sharp knife deeper into my back. The doctor's recommendation was pain killer and bed rest. During this period I missed four weeks of school, and a substitute was called in to teach my classes. On one occasion, I was in bed with Sparky lying along my right leg, her butt nearest me. I was reading the chapter in Stephen King's *Pet Sematary* in which the main character, Louis Creed, gets out of the bathtub or shower and is shocked to see Churchill, the cat, reincarnated and sitting, as I recall, behind the toilet seat.

Churchill had been run over by a tractor trailer. I believe Louis kicks at the cat out of horror/exasperation, and at that precise moment, Sparky turned very slowly and stared at me. I held the book but was no longer reading. I just kept looking at Sparky as she stared at me. Then I carefully closed the book and placed it on the stand next to our bed. I felt at that moment Sparky knew what had happened to Churchill, and she disapproved.

When I would come home from school, I often took an afternoon nap and once I was settled Sparky would come up and curl in next to my chest and sleep with me. When I felt lousy, this action was especially comforting, although sometimes I had the strange thought that her heart rhythm might somehow throw my heart rhythm off, and I would have a heart attack.

As happens to many cats who are aging, her kidneys began to fail and the last few months were painful — anyone who has had a pet for a long period of time knows this. Debbie would bring her outside to a blanket on the lawn. She would rest in the sun for a while, then start back to the house, almost crawling — a few paces and she'd stop, a few more paces and she'd stop. Debbie would get up as Sparky neared the steps and help her up and into the house.

We saw her take her last breath on the floor between the kitchen and the dining room. We said a prayer, and Debbie went off to work, a choice she later regretted. My job was to take Sparky to the vets and arrange for a cremation. I remember as I put her in the cardboard box that her body was already getting stiff. The ashes arrived a few weeks later, and we buried her with a piece of her blanket (wrapped in plastic) in the back yard under a pine tree. Sometime shortly after, we bought a stone statue of St. Francis, the patron saint of animals, and placed it near the grave. That was followed a year later with a stone statue of a cat that now sits over the gravesite.

And that was it. My wife said that she couldn't deal with the loss of another creature and so there would be no more pets.

I had known Kristen, a young Spanish teacher in our school, for a few years and even had the privilege of traveling down to her family's farm in Cooperstown with Brother Joe Fragala and visiting for the day. We had breakfast in a diner the family ran and then we got a tour of the farm, particularly the cow barns. Sal, her affable father, loved showing the city slickers around the farm. I guess I was a city slicker, even though I had spent the first seven years of my life on a farm. I do remember that there seemed to be animals running around everywhere — chickens, cats, dogs, geese, maybe even a goat or two.

On a number of occasions back at school, Kristen would show me a picture of a kitten and say, "Wouldn't you and Debbie like a cat?" I would tell her that I didn't think so and that Debbie had such a hard time with the loss of Sparky that she didn't want to deal with another cat. But Kristen kept trying and got lucky one summer day.

"Hey, guess what?" I had picked up the phone on a summer morning to hear Kristen's question.

"What's up?"

"My mom and sister are driving up from Cooperstown with a cat for you."

And before I could speak, she added, "Here is what you need to do. Go to the pet store and buy two bowls, for food and water, a litter box, litter, and some food that is appropriate for kittens."

"Listen, Turkey, I told you we don't want a cat. Debbie is not ready for one now — and maybe not ever."

"I know, but would you at least come and look at it," she whined.

"Okay. I do want to say hello to your mother and Amanda."

"Good. By the way, this cat has three legs."

"Are you serious? If we were to get a cat, it would have four legs. Come on, really!"

I entered the kitchen to the hellos and hugs of Amanda and Jeanne and then they signaled me to turn around. Leaning up against the refrigerator and looking up at me was this little three-legged black creature. It was over.

"Ok, what do I need to get? Food, litter box ..." and they burst into laughter. "We knew you couldn't resist once you saw him."

"Does he have a name?"

"Sidecar, Stumpy," said Amanda, laughing.

"I don't think so," I said. "By the way, what happened to his back leg?"

"Well," Kristen's Mom began, "I think the cord wrapped around the leg in the womb and choked off the blood supply. When she gave birth to this one, the leg was pretty much dead."

I was holding him now and could feel the absence of the back leg. "Well, let's see how he does. I can't believe I said yes and haven't even talked to Debbie."

Debbie entered from the garage and walked through the kitchen. I stood inside and said nothing. "What's going on?"

I must have given something away because she looked to her right and there was the little black cat on the sofa — I had placed him there — looking right at her. "What is this?" she asked.

"Well, it's a cat. The Licatas brought the cat up from the farm for us."

Debbie was near the sofa and reached down and picked him up.

"He is missing a back leg, but he is quite a little guy." She sat down on the sofa, and he moved his body to adjust. She began talking to him. "Now, tell me about yourself, you little creature." Within five minutes, their friendship was established.

Shortly after, I proposed the name CT, short for Cooperstown, the town he had come from. Debbie liked the name immediately, and so the little black cat, now officially CT, became part of our life.

When he walks, his limp is severely pronounced, but when he runs, the limp disappears and he is super-fast. Whether chasing balls Debbie throws or playing hide and seek with her, he can fly with the best of cats. I have even seen him jump in the air and catch a ball with his two front paws. They have become great pals and like most really good buddies have their rituals. In the morning, after giving CT breakfast, she brews her tea, prepares her cereal, and heads for favorite chair in the study. To the chair, she has attached little toys on strings. CT ducks under the chair, pops out whichever side she dangles a toy from, bats it around, or pulls it down to work over with his three legs. Eventually he goes behind the chair and catches his first snooze of the day.

When I enter the bedroom late at night — I am a night owl — CT is almost always asleep between Debbie's legs. Once I get in and get my body into position to sleep, he awakes. As I turn the light off, he gets up and leaves. I could get an inferiority complex about this, but I rationalize that I have put some of his food out before going to bed, and he is going to have a night snack.

One moment with CT I viewed as a bit of a shocker at first and then as a kind of miracle. CT was in his fifth year with us — he is now in his ninth. Christmas season and the house was decorated. On the top of a bookcase near the stairs, we had placed our wooden manger set, with all the essential figures, a set which we had had for years. As I walked out into the living room one morning, I saw on the floor a lamb — part of the manger set but it looked odd. When I bent down to pick it up, I noticed that it was missing a back leg — and there on the floor was the back leg. It had been chewed off. I looked at CT and spoke angrily, "What is wrong with you? We have had this set for years. Why did you do this?" I stared at the figure's missing leg. CT slowly walked out to the back room and then looked back at me. As I looked at CT, it hit me. The more I thought about it, the more fantastic and miraculous and true it seemed. He had done that so that he, a three-legged animal, could be represented at the birth of Christ. Since that day, he has never touched another piece of the set, and every year very much present with the other animals looking down at the baby Jesus is the three-legged lamb.

"Who's the Toughest Kid in Town?"

Some thought the toughest kid in town was Kenny. Some thought it was Allan. A few thought it might be me. A couple of kids were unknowns regarding their fighting abilities. But in a small town like Raymertown, with the number of boys in the 9 to 12 age ranging about 13 or so — if you counted a couple of guys from the back roads — eventually it gets sorted out.

At the far end of the village lived an Italian family, the only one in the village. Dickie was about my size, and his fighting ability was unknown. One summer day, four or five of us were in the school yard standing near a swing, and I was about to take my turn when Dickie shoved me and said, "I'm next." I grabbed his arm and said, "No, I was next." He said something like, "Get back," and shoved me. And suddenly we were wrestling — the secret of wrestling in a small village where reputation is key is that you don't want to end up on the bottom. And the next secret is that if you get the other person down and you have a headlock in place, the game is over. I hadn't actually squeezed that hard when I heard him say, "I give up. Stop."

Andre was a big kid, his family new to our town. One night at Ward's Field, after a game of baseball, Allan, the son of the owner of the field, challenged Andre to a wrestling match. I kind of felt sorry for Andre — new kid and all — I knew that Allan was one rugged guy, stocky and strong. After a few preliminary words and shoves, they engaged. Allan sort of half picked Andre up and body slammed him. Andre stayed on the ground, head down, waving off any further engagement.

Kenny was wiry and fast and tough. I did not see his fight with Allan, wrestling with some boxing thrown in, but those who saw the engagement said that Allan beat Kenny in a close fight, though Roy, Kenny's brother, still argued that Kenny had won.

And so, leaving out the others — Roy, Rich, Dale, George, Elmer, Charlie, and my brother John — we were down to two: Allan and me. The stage, this time in our back yard, was set to determine the Toughest Fighter in Raymertown. There would be an audience of one, my brother John.

Boxing was the sport of choice, using two sets of boxing gloves that John and I had been given by my cousins. John, orchestrating the event, would be ring designer, bell ringer, referee, and my corner man.

The clothes line was attached to a bush by the outhouse, then stretched to a pointed stick we had pounded into the ground, then to the handle of the cellar door, and finally to a big nail along the side of the woodshed. It was a pretty loose ring with a very odd shape.

Allan had on just his bathing suit, his upper body strong and heavy, head almost shaved. I wore a white t-shirt, maybe to conceal my skin and bones, and jeans. John signaled us to opposite corners. "Ok, he said, "Two rounds, two minutes each round." He held a pot upside down in one hand and a spoon in the other. He glanced at his wrist watch, looked at Allan and looked at me — why did he look scared? Then he banged the pot with the spoon, said, "Go!" and dropped the pot and spoon just outside the rope.

My head exploded with a thousand bursting stars — Allan had charged out and thrown the first punch. The stars kept bursting and bursting, but I was still standing, holding on to Allan. John stepped between us — gave me a major look of concern and shoved Allan back. I tried to slide behind John to avoid any more explosions. I ducked and wove and slid and nearly dove, feeling bursts of air racing by me and hearing his awful grunts. And then John starting banging the pot. "Round one is over." Thank Almighty God.

The second round, cut from two minutes to under one by the timekeeper, showed me to be a master of elusiveness. Roger the Dodger Staubach could have learned some moves from me that day. Allan chased, I ran, and dodged. The bell — deus ex machina.

John looked at Allen and then looked at me. "I going to have to call this fight a draw." Allan uttered the equivalent of WTF in the 50's — probably a line like "This is a lotta horseshit." And I just sighed knowing that I had avoided getting knocked out and maybe even killed.

But in a small town, especially when there are two to one odds, the word gets out that there are now two people one shouldn't mess with: Allan Ward and Yours Truly.

"The Fastest Wheels in Town?"

I am not sure where Mom and Dad came up with the money — maybe there had been a special sale, maybe someone had helped them with the gift — but there it was, and not even my birthday: a new bike and, best of all, an English bike. I had been talking for some time about these cool bikes I had seen an ad for — stylish, sleek, fast, and with three speeds. And somehow my wish had come true. A miracle.

My father, of course, had a huge smile as I walked around the bike touching it as if it were something exotic and precious. Black with gold lettering and white trim, narrow tires designed for speed, handlebar brakes, and a gear shift on the right side of the handlebar, just above the hand grip. I stood next to it, used my right foot to move the kickstand back, and climbed aboard — a little unsteady, but I focused and straightened the wheel and moved out onto the road in front of our house. I had read about the gears, that you needed to stop pedaling to shift, and so I stopped and shifted into second, and felt the change immediately in my leg muscles. I turned around by the barn near the main highway and headed back toward the house. I wanted to reach enough speed to shift into third. I pedaled faster and then paused, shifting into third — back down with the feet, and I was starting to really fly. I slowed down near the hill leading up to a neighbor's house and headed back to the starting point. What a bike, I thought. What a great gift.

In a small village, word gets around fast, and the truth among one's peers is that new machines and equipment need to be tested and challenged. That night, still early evening, I rode my bike down into the village. In front of Odd Fellows' Hall, a small group of boys had gathered to check the bike out. Kenny was the one to make the challenge: "You say that bike is supposed to be so fast. How about tomorrow night at 7? We race from the top of Ford's Hill to the Lutheran Church." I didn't feel confident or at all skilled on the bike, but the challenge was there, made right in front of four other guys. "Yeah, ok, I'll give it a shot," I said.

Ford's Hill is named after a farmer who owned the land the town highway went through. We would start on a relatively flat section of blacktop highway. The road would move into a slow but brief curve to the left, then straighten out a bit and drop down at roughly a forty-five degree angle, level out briefly, and then drop dramatically down to the bottom of the hill, where another town road merged from the left. It was at the foot of the hill, at the merger point, where the bicyclist had to make a dramatic and awkward cutback to the merging road from the village. Once on this road, it was a straight shot to the Lutheran Church — less than a quarter of a mile.

I can't remember who was at the starting line to signal go. A couple of guys would ride behind us, there was one guy at the cutback corner, and the rest of the guys were at the finish line.

Kenny was off ahead of me. I was still in first gear and was shifting to second, but he was pedaling furiously in the only gear he had. By the time I had reached high gear, we were nearing the slow curve. And it was on the curve I caught up with him. We were now flying. I had pulled ahead as we leveled out and were about to make the first drop.

As I raced downhill, my eyes filled with water — I had never given a thought to goggles. Then leveling out, I got ready for the big drop. As I came over the top, I felt both exhilarated and terrified. Heading down the last steep section of highway, I was maybe ten-twelve lengths ahead, but now I was heading toward big trouble. There was no way I was going to stay on my bicycle at this speed and navigate the turn. Half way down, I squeezed the brakes, let up, squeezed them again — I might crash even slowing down. And then Kenny raced by on my left, standing and screaming something like "Yeeehaaaa." He had gotten the inside position and didn't hit his brakes until 70 feet or so from the turn — his bike went into a long skid, the back tire slid out to the right, and then he jerked up on the handlebars, and to my amazement, his bike ended up facing the Lutheran Church. I had made a very wide turn, ending up off the road in some rough turf and grass. Dale, who had been standing by a tree, ran toward me yelling, "Jesus, Paul, go! Go! Go!"

Kenny was thirty yards ahead of me before I could regain the road and full strength. I made up a little distance before the end, but the race was over. He was standing by his bike with a smile on his face as I crossed the imaginary line. On this night, the new bike in town did not pass the test that would have earned it the title of "Fastest Bike in Town."

There Were Always Sports

There were always sports when we were growing up, and because I had a brother relatively close in age, we always had at least a starting point, one against one. As season melted into season, we would shift to the next sport and select the appropriate equipment.

Spring brought baseball. On the radio in our house, it was the Brooklyn Dodgers and their wonderful cast of players — Jackie Robinson, Roy Campanella, Pee Wee Reese, Duke Snider, Johnny Padres, and the rest of the Boys of Summer. In the village of Raymertown, there were Allan Ward, Roy Bornt and his brother Kenny, Rich Meron, George Wagner, Dale Cushman, Elmer Crow, Charlie Barry, Dave Garafano, and the two O'Brien boys. Our games were usually after dinner until dusk, and the setting for most of the games was Wards' Field, the Wards' front yard. Most of the time, it ended up four against four with each player having multiple duties — the pitcher often covered first, for example. Pitcher, catcher, infielder and outfielder — that pretty much did it. What gave the game constant tension — at least when certain batters were up — was the fact that Route 7, a busy highway, framed the outfield. Usually we had the outfielder stand at the guard rail and look up the road to see if cars were coming; if they weren't or weren't close, he would yell, "Go." On a number of occasions over the years, the outfielder would forget to yell and the ball would sail up and over the road, but not always over — the sound of a car being hit was a horrible moment. Sometimes the cars would keep going; at other times, you could hear the sound of squealing brakes, and the drivers would pull over into the lot next to Baker's Garage, get out, look at the car, fire off a few curse words combined with some verbal gestures in our direction, and then tear off. I remember a few times when the brakes screeched particularly loudly; then we raced behind Ward's house and hid in the heavy undergrowth.

It was in baseball that my brother had two brief and disappointing runs at organized sports. John's first attempt was to try out for the Center Brunswick Little League, but he was told on arrival that our home in Raymertown was out of the Little League district. In high school John had a much better initial experience, but the playing field was not level. During the first day of practice trying out for junior varsity baseball, John performed well. In the infield, he fielded six grounders smoothly and in each case fired the ball right to first base. At bat, he lined the ball for what would have been hits four or five times in his ten attempts at the plate. He felt good about what he had showed the coach. When the players reached the field house after practice, the team roster was posted. "Looked as if the coaches had already selected their team or they did some pretty speedy calculating," said my brother.

Moving into summer: Though we did not view swimming as a sport, it was a crucial part of our summers. Summers were so hot. I remember how excited we were when my father installed a fan in the kitchen window. At least dinner could be consumed with a breeze wafting across the brow. But the days were brutal, and we found some relief in the stream behind our house. John and I and whoever else we could muster up would build our own swimming pools by damming up the stream. I am not sure where we got the burlap bags which we filled with sod taken from the stream's banks, but about 25 bags or so created enough backup to give us a pool four or five feet deep. With a few inner tubes, we found our summer relief in our own creation.

There are two moments that involved swimming that are vivid memories. The first was at Camp Tekakwitha. I was the only one in Cabin 17 who was not a swimmer, and so when we went down to the lake to swim, I had to stay in the intermediate section, roped off and filled with younger campers. I was determined to become a swimmer, and so I signed up to take the test.

To pass the test, you had to swim from the dock to a raft about 100 feet out in the lake, touch the raft, and swim back to the dock — twice. I had to do it!!. With a counselor on the dock and one on the raft, I dove into the water. Now, my actual swimming skills were severely limited — I could do about four strokes, but I didn't really know how to do them well without getting my mouth filled with water, and so I would resort to the old dog paddle. I was tired when I reached the raft, where the counselor shouted, "Ok, O'Brien - first part done!!" And I started back toward the dock which looked a mile away. My arms felt heavy and the forward progress was so slow. I had to stop now; there was no way I could do it again. But when I reached the dock, the other counselor yelled, "Go, O'Brien, you're more than half way there!" I started back, tried a few strokes with arms that were dead weights that quickly dropped into the water. I remember thinking that I might go under and figured that at least someone would see me and rescue me. If I had known Jon Krakauer's line as he descended Everest in the storm — "Keep it together" — I would have tried that, but the best I could do, and it was a good one was, "Jesus, help me." I don't remember touching the raft, but I do remember hearing, "You're almost there." The dock was Paris, and I was in New York. No feeling left in my arms — I was more or less bobbing on the water. You'll never get there. Never get there. Well, I thought, at least you tried. And then I felt myself sinking, getting cold, and about to give it all up but with one last effort I drove my legs into the water and reached up desperately with my right arm and felt something hard — wood — the dock. I had made it. I had reached the dock. I was too weak to pull myself up, and the counselor reached down and hoisted me up. I couldn't stand and collapsed on the dock in total exhaustion. "Hey," the counselor said, "you made it, O'Brien." When I wrote a note to my parents that night, I proudly announced that I was a swimmer.

The other swimming moment occurred at Lake Lorraine, a small, popular lake outside the village of Pittstown. John and I had traveled there with my sister and her boyfriend Colin, who would eventually become her husband. I was with John and a few other kids in a nearby pavilion, which featured a small concession stand and a few pinball machines, when we heard the shouts and screams. We raced back to see my sister and Colin being rescued from the middle of the lake. As I recall there were three guys who dove in to save them. Later, I found out what had happened. Colin, who was a good swimmer, had talked my sister into going out into deeper water with him. Rose had a basic fear of water but was persuaded to go out with Colin — no worries, he would take care of her. Then she panicked. At first Colin tried to laugh it off, but she started thrashing and pushing him under, causing him to swallow water. The guys on shore saw what was going on, dove in, and were able to save the two of them. One image sticks with me, that of a soaked wallet on a towel. One of the men had not hesitated a second at all to dive in for the rescue.

To my knowledge, there was only one person in our village who had a set of golf clubs, the funeral director's son. Although we had heard about heroes like Bobby Jones, Ben Hogan, and Slamming Sammy Snead, John and I did not really know or appreciate the sport of golf. John, barely a teenager, had caddied at the Troy Country Club one warm summer day without understanding one thing about golf. "Go up there and spot the ball for me," the golfer said to John. On top of the small hill, John said, "Yeah, I see it." The golfer shouted, "About a 7 iron to the pin?" John had no idea what that meant, but said, "Sounds just about right." John's career as caddy ended that day. On another occasion a few years later, I had finished my morning/lunch shift at the Hot Shoppes in Albany and picked John up at St. Mary's Hospital where he was working as an orderly. I am not sure who said it, but one of us said, "Hey, how about a round of golf?" Frear Park was a course we knew, John more so since he and few friends at Our Lady of Victory used to sneak onto one of the holes during lunch hour and find golf balls, some that had just been hit. This day oddly enough, we both looked alike, white shirts with black pants. I think we also were wearing work shoes. In the club house, I am sure we were viewed as the rawest amateurs as we rented small golf bags that held four clubs and then purchased a bag of used balls. I don't remember how bad we were, but I do know that as we headed for the fifth tee, a hard rain began to fall, and we decided to return to the club house. Doesn't take much imagination to see the comic picture of two young "uniformed" guys thoroughly soaked carrying pathetic golf bags on their way back to the club house. When we walked in, John even had the nerve to ask the pro if we got a discount. "Nope," the guy said, "that's it for you guys."

Fast forward twenty-five years to a gorgeous summer day and a vastly different venue than Frear Park. Our foursome is about to tee off on the tenth hole of the Pines Course at Seaview Golf Resort just north of Atlantic City. Approaching from behind us is a golf cart with two men in tuxes, the passenger now waving to us. They pull up. "Is this the Nadeau party?" the passenger asks. Colin, my brother-in-law, laughs and says, "That would be us." Both men exit the cart and step behind it where one opens a cooler and takes out a bottle of champagne; the other reaches into the cooler and takes out four champagne glasses. He hands one to each of us, and the other pours the champagne. "Gentlemen," the driver says, "here's to a great game," lifting his hand to simulate a drink, and then we lift our glasses and drink. As the two tuxedoed men drive off, I feel as if I have just been in a scene from *The Great Gatsby*.

Starting some time in the mid '80s, the three O'Brien brothers were the recipients of some pretty special treatment at Seaview Golf Resort located just north of Atlantic City. The reason we were able to move into this rarified air was that Colin, my brother-in-law, a long time Marriott employee, had become New England Regional Vice-President, and Seaview was one of his properties. For three days and two nights, we felt like royalty. A limo into Atlantic City for dinner and then a show and some gambling; the finest treatment and wines whenever we dined at the resort; golf jackets and shirts with the Seaview Logo; and constant attention wherever we went. Yes, royalty. Our game had improved to the degree that we were respectable on their challenging courses: the Pines and the Bay. Colin took care of all expenses; no question he had a good rate at the hotel, but Colin is by nature a generous person, and when he is with people he cares about, money is never an issue. In a real way, from the beginning he has been our brother.

Fall was football, and the memory of my disappointing attempt to join organized sports. The weekend before freshman football tryouts, I had talked my parents into taking me to the Army-Navy store to buy football cleats (recommended in the notice we had gotten from the school about tryouts). Because money was tight, my parents suggested a used pair of cleats, but for me "used" didn't matter. Used cleats were gold to me.

"You got cleats?" Freddie said to me in the hallway. Standing in front of a very popular and for me intimidating classmate, I mumbled, "Yeah." He looked around, "What size?" I responded, "Nine." He put his arm on my shoulder and looked at me. "Ok, that works. Today, I'll use your cleats, and you can wear my sneakers. Ok?" I nodded yes.

As I turned to make a cut on the rain-swept field, I slipped and fell. I tried again and again and kept falling. The field was just too wet, and a killer for those who didn't have cleats. Unlike the experience of my brother, it wasn't until the following day that I saw the list of those who had made the team. I wasn't on it; Freddie was. He did return my cleats eventually once he had gotten his new pair, and he played four years of football.

There were pick-up games in the village of Raymertown and in our back yard, usually tackle and with little or no equipment. For a while I had a leather helmet, which pretty much offered no protection, except for keeping my head dry when we played in the rain. If we were lucky, we might through word of mouth be able to get five or six guys and have a pretty good game. Sometimes the game was just me against my brother John. Because I was older and bigger, I used to take his snap — each of us snapped to the other — and run straight ahead seeing how far I could go with John on my back. As I would run, I would say, "Alan 'the Horse Ameche' cannot be stopped."

Neither could Bob Pettit from the corner! I was Bob Pettit, and I was shooting over Bob Cousy, my brother John, for the score. Hoop! Our court was the driveway into the garage and the adjacent lawn. The driveway made a fairly sharp turn just outside the foul line if you were heading into the garage. During the fall season and even sometimes in the winter, when shoveling was sometimes necessary, John and I played a lot of one on one games, a lot of twenty-one, and a lot of OUT. When players came who were strangers to our court, we had a huge advantage. On one occasion, I had two friends visiting from college, both of whom had played high school hoop. In a little pick-up game to 21, John and I beat them handily. We knew where the odd bounces were and where the ball would go when it hit that particular corner of the pavement. Home court advantage!

Once the snows had come, we had our afternoon routine. Arriving home from school in the 3:30 p.m. range, we would change quickly, grab a shovel, skates and hockey sticks, and head up to Kilt's Pond, a small pond located down the hill from a faded-red farm house of an odd couple, Grace and Myron, who were forerunners to non-married couples living together. We would quickly shovel a rink; once done we would lace up our skates, create goals with pine branches, and battle each other. We would play until darkness had fallen.

On February 4, 1980, *The New Yorker*'s cover captured our ice-skating world: A drawing of a pond where two boys, one tightening his laces, the other waiting, appear to be preparing to play hockey. Bare trees frame the pond, and on the hill above the pond, one can see the top section of a barn with a house nearby. I stared at the picture and thought how close the drawing seemed to our world. I immediately drove to the local news stand and bought two more copies. I carefully removed two of the covers, framed one for myself, framed one for my brother, and kept one magazine in its entirety. The next time I visited my brother in Boston, I gave him the framed picture of our hockey world.

When sports play a major role in your life, it's inevitable that you have your favorite role models and teams. For me, the Dodgers, the Celtics, and the New York Giants were at the top: the Dodgers with Jackie Robinson and Roy Campanella as underdogs in their epic battles in the 50's with the New York Yankees; the Celtics with Bob Cousy and Bill Russell; the Giants with Frank Gifford and Charlie Conerly — to this moment, I still remember standing with my father and two brothers in front of the television on December 28, 1958, desperately hoping that Johnny Unitas would make a mistake as the Colts drove toward the Giants' end zone in overtime, and the final hammer when one of my backyard heroes — Alan Ameche — scored on a 1-yard touchdown run to give the Colts the NFL Championship, 23-17.

Over time, certain favorites waned, and I developed interest in new teams. The Dodgers left town, and perhaps because I was going to college in New Rochelle, I started following the Yankees. The New York Knickerbockers with Bill Bradley and Walt Frazier became my NBA team as they drove toward their most magical era — the early 70's. But one team always remained constant: Notre Dame University's Fighting Irish — with sparkling epithets like the "Four Horsemen" and "Seven Mules" and the phrase "Win one for the Gipper"; and with magical names — Gus Dorais, Knute Rockne, George Gipp, Johnny Lujack, Frank Leahy, and Terry Brennan. It was during the Terry

Brennan coaching era that I found the Irish on the radio and listened to every game I could catch. I remember that 1956 was a very bad year with only two wins, but one of the players became my hero — Paul Hornung, handsome, rugged, a battler — even winning the Heisman Trophy that horrible year. The following year Notre Dame scored one of the biggest upsets in sports' history by defeating the Oklahoma Sooners, a team that had won 47 consecutive games.

In 2010 I got my big chance. At Kentucky Derby Day at Notre Dame-Bishop Gibbons School, I bid on 4 tickets to the Notre Dame-Purdue game, which would kick off the 2010 season. As I remember, the ticket bidding was intense, and I had the final bid at somewhere in the range of 500 dollars. For the first time, I would see the Fighting Irish live in South Bend, Indiana. So many memories, so many emotions that were part of my history with this team — I could feel them rushing forward.

I drove to my sister and brother-in-law's home in Andover, and Colin and I flew out of Manchester-Boston Airport heading to Chicago on Friday, September 3. My brother John would fly out later from Logan. The three of us met John's son Eamon in Chicago, where he had booked us rooms at a downtown Marriott. Saturday morning we would be on the road to South Bend.

The seats were on the 50 yard line but high up in the very top row, our backs pressed firmly against the solid concrete wall behind us. I had heard about the hospitality that takes place at South Bend, and it far exceeded my expectations. Everywhere there were warm welcomes — from the bus driver who drove us in from the parking lot to the bookstore employees to the ushers at the Stadium — and I felt at home.

At roughly 3 p.m. with the Irish fight song revved up, the leprechaun emerged from the tunnel carrying the ND banner, followed by first year coach Brian Kelly, and then the team. I could feel my mind and body just becoming overwhelmed — all those years — and the tears of joy started, and then I felt my brother's elbow in my ribs. "Give me your soda," he said. With tears pouring down, I said, "Why?" He said, "Pass it over," and despite the signs everywhere that said, "No Alcohol," he took from his coat a flask of Jameson's and poured a shot into my coke. "You're going to need this!" he said. The final score that day was Notre Dame 23 - Purdue 12.

The Trophy

Like many teachers, I do have certain stories that keep coming back, touchstone stories, stories that I knew I would tell my students at some point during the year. Stories about lessons I have learned. One key story goes back to the summer between my seventh and eighth grades, and the setting for the story was Camp Tekakwitha and a summer program sponsored by the Albany Catholic Diocese. The most recent occasion of my telling of this story was at the Notre Dame-Bishop Gibbons 2016 National Honor Society Dinner. I began at the dinner by talking a little bit about my role as an honor student.

In high school, I was a top-notch student in American History class. When I would get home from school, my mother would ask me how my day went. "Got 20 out of 20 on a history quiz," I'd say in a low-key fashion. "Good," she would respond, but when the report card came and I had a 74 in history, she looked at me and said, "Didn't you tell me you were doing well in history!" The truth was I was doing well in history class. My good friend Jimmy Reilly and I sat next to each other in the back of the room, and we gave each other weekly tests on sports' trivia. On a particular day, we would exchange quizzes in the back of the room, and I often scored 20 out of 20 on his. I nailed Bob Pettit as the NBA MVP of 1956; I knew that the punch that made Kid Gavilan a special fighter was the bolo punch; and that Alan "the Horse" Ameche was the 1954 Heisman Trophy winner — after all, I had become "the Horse" in the back yard running against my brother whom I had named Howard "Hopalong" Cassidy, the Heisman winner of 1955. I mean these were great characters from the history of sports.

Sometimes in our lives, it is hard to see beyond our immediate needs and desires: we forge ahead in our own worlds, often oblivious to other things around us, things we should be paying attention to. Like the old story David Foster Wallace told at the Kenyon College Commencement Address in 2005. "There are these two young fish swimming along, and they happen to meet an older fish swimming the other way, who nods at them and says, 'Morning, boys. How's the water?' And the two young fish swim on for a bit, and eventually one of them looks over at the other and goes, 'What the hell is water?'" (3-4). Yes, we are often in it, but we don't see it.

A little bit like the time I received my first honor. Let me take you back to 1956. I am in a two-week summer program the Albany Diocese has sponsored for youth during the summer season at Camp Tekakwitha, located on Lake Luzerne. There are four two-week sessions with approximately 200 kids in each one. I am in Cabin 17 with thirteen other boys, and we are the first cabin in the senior division which numbers 17-21. Fortunately our cabin has many good athletes, and we have done well in the athletic competition — we are tied for first place in the senior division. As I head off to sleep on a Thursday night — three days before returning home — I am musing on tomorrow's championship baseball game against Cabin 21. I am our team's center fielder, and I often imagine myself as Duke Snider, the Brooklyn Dodgers' center fielder, and my hero. The winner of tomorrow's championship game gets to go on an over-night canoe hike.

Someone is tapping on my shoulder — it's very late. "O'Brien!" I look and it's one of the camp counselors. "Come outside," he says. "Get a move on." I crawl out of my bed in my pjs and step outside the cabin, where two other counselors have joined the first. They have flashlights. "Ok," one says, "do twenty pushups." I am in pretty good shape, so twenty is not difficult, but I am bewildered. "Twenty jumping jacks," the second counselor says, and I do twenty. And then the one who woke me says, "Do twenty sit-ups." I do them. And then I stand. "You ok, O'Brien?"

he asks. I look at him and though I am in a complete fog about what is going on, I say, "Sure." He smiles and says, "Back to bed, my man. We will see you in the morning."

The bugle blows at seven signaling wake-up. We dress and talk about the big game, then head for the dining hall. On the way back to the cabin to get our baseball equipment, I hear my name called, "O'Brien." It's the same counselor who got me out of bed, and he is approaching me. "Come with me," he says.

"I can't," I say. "I have to get ready for the big game."

"You're not playing," he says. "You have other things to do."

Stunned, I say, "But I'm our center fielder."

"They'll make do," he says. "Follow me."

We are heading down a dirt path through the woods which ends at the beach and boathouse. Against the side of the boathouse is a rake, and the counselor reaches for it and hands it to me. "You can start by raking the beach" and points to a specific spot. He turns and heads back up the path disappearing into the woods.

Just a few minutes into the task, the whole experience catches ahold of me, and I feel my body shaking and the tears start to flow. "Hey there, what's going on?" A voice — and I turn to another counselor who has emerged from the boathouse. He approaches me, putting out his hand and saying, "I'm Tom and you are?" I tell him and then he asks me what is going on. I recount the morning's start, and he listens. "Well, Paul," he begins speaking gently and thoughtfully about the challenges life can offer us, often ones we don't completely understand, and I am listening and sort of hearing because what is really coming across is the caring in the voice that I hear. When he finishes talking, I feel calmer, like the way you feel after a long exhale. And then he says, "You can probably help me with a couple of boats when you finish up with the beach. Besides, I'd love to have someone to chat with."

I finish raking and am now in the boathouse — sanding the underside of my second row boat — while chatting with Tom who is painting another boat that is standing upright — when I hear a commotion of noise from the woods. My cabin. They won the game and are heading out in canoes for the overnight. A couple of them wave to me as I stand in the doorway of the boathouse. Then they and the rest get in canoes and head out. I feel a little sad and disappointed but not the way I had before.

Later that day, I am asked to help clean and organize stuff in the canteen, kind of like a small store. It is at the end of this task that the counselor who had awakened me and took me to the beach walks into the canteen. I decide to go for it and ask him why I ended up here rather than on the canoe hike.

"You were selected as this session's honor camper for the senior division. Today was all about proving that you were worthy, and you did a pretty good job, Paul."

Flash forward five months. At the Cardinal McCloskey High School gym, campers from all four summer sessions have gathered for an afternoon end-of-year celebration. It's a day of games, laughter, and food. After a couple of hours of fun, we are all asked to take a seat for the award ceremony. Awards are given for different skills mastered in the summer and certificates are given out for winners in the sports' division. The last award is "Honor Camper of the Year."

Starting with number 5, each runner-up is called to the awards' table for a certificate and a small gift. As they reach number 3, I happen to glance down at the open doors leading out of the gym. In the doorway stands Tom, the counselor in the boathouse. He sees me, smiles and then winks. "And now for the Honor Camper of the Year — he is from the Senior Division, Session 3, Cabin 17 — Paul O'Brien." Both dazed and elated, I stumble down the bleachers and shake hands with the Bishop and the head of the program, Father Delaney, while local photographers snap pictures.

After, I run all the way to the car where my father waits. He is thrilled at my award, which reads "Paul O'Brien, Cabin 17, Honor Camper of the Year."

As a little coda to this moment of achievement, a few years later, I returned home on a break from college and while relaxing in the living room, I noticed that my trophy was not in its familiar shelf overlooking my father's easy chair. I went to my Mom.

"Heh, Mom, what happened to my trophy?"

"Oh dear," she said, "I was dusting and knocked it off the shelf."

"Mom, It's the only trophy I have ever won in my life — and you broke it. Where is it?"

"Well, the top part was in many pieces — so I threw them out. I did save the base."

"Oh well, at least I have part of it."

Many years later when Brother Bill Cronin at the high school heard my story, he came into my classroom the following day, carrying a trophy — an old debate club trophy. "I thought you needed a trophy," he said, "a whole trophy."

When I reflect on this camp experience today, a few things come to mind: the confusion and bewilderment I felt, the pain and sadness of not being part of something, the joy, after some time, of winning the big prize and my happiness and pride in showing my parents, but most of all when I think about this moment, I remember the comforting voice of Tom. And his smile and his wink and most of all, I remember his kindness.

Cheapskate

"Boys, the Kellys are here. Come down and say hello," said my mother at the foot of the stairs. The Kellys were the last people my brother John and I wanted to see. "Boys," she called again, and we knew that we had to make an appearance.

A week earlier, my father had asked us if we wanted to make some money, and we had both eagerly responded yes. Money was kind of scarce in our lives, though we never felt poor. "The Kellys are doing a major cleaning of their house, and they need some help. I told them that you guys might be interested." The Kellys were family friends down the road about five miles, and would drop in to say hello to my parents every so often — they had two sons who were priests, and my brother was a priest, so there was plenty of common ground.

My father dropped us off at 8 in the morning, and Mrs. Kelly had work ready to go. She told us that it would be indoors in the morning with her; outdoors in the afternoon with Mr. Kelly. Mrs. K, dark glasses, a band tied around her hair, and a serious demeanor: "Boys, I want the walls washed down, the windows cleaned, the hardwood floors mopped thoroughly, first upstairs and then downstairs, then we need to go into the attic and tidy up a bit — it's a disaster up there, but it can wait, if you don't get to it." We went to work. It was mid-summer, but she had a couple of good fans that we could maneuver in front of us when we got too hot. She slipped in and out looking at our work and offering a little advice — "missed a couple of spots on the third pane of the window," "run the mop way into the corner," and occasionally, "nice work, boys."

Then it was lunch. Tuna sandwiches and milk. "Guys, you will be out with me this afternoon," Mr. Kelly said, "Plenty to do — got some raking, some trimming, some lumber needs to be moved in the barn, and, oh yeah, you have to do the outside windows too — let's do the windows first. I have some ladders ready to go."

We went to work again. Windows, hedge and bush trimming, raking, but we didn't really feel the heat until we got in the barn and started moving lumber. No relief and no cool breezes. We kept at it, following Mr. Kelly's directives. And then we heard the magic words — "Ok, boys, I think that is going to do it for the day."

We stood outside in the sun, and he said, "Paul, here is some money for your day's work." I approached him, and reached for bills he handed to me tightly folded so that I could not see the number of the bill. Then he called John over and handed him bills also tightly folded. "Thank you, boys. Your Pop picking you up?" We said no, that we were going to hitchhike home.

Out of sight of the Kelly house, we both reached in our pockets and took out our salary for the day. I couldn't believe it — two single dollar bills, tightly folded together. Disbelief. "What?" John had the same reaction. "This can't be it," I said. I had dreamed of holding a twenty or at least a ten in my hand. John looked at the two bucks in his hand, "Eight hours of work — and two bucks — he may be the cheapest guy on earth."

We entered our house, looking like two street urchins out of *Oliver*. "Well," my mother said, "how did it all go?" I looked at John and then at my Mom. "Mr. Kelly is really cheap." She stared at me. "A whole day of work," I said, "and he gave us a lousy two bucks each." She looked out the window at the state highway, "Well, you each have two dollars more than when you started the day. Did Mrs. Kelly give you lunch?" John burst out, "Yeah, a tuna fish sandwich and milk — not even chips." My mother had had it, "Ok, that's enough. Be thankful for the money you have."

Then the Kellys had popped in to see Mom and Dad. Of course, they had no idea of how John and I had bad-mouthed them to each other all week about our pathetic pay. The Kellys and my parents were seated at the table when we entered the kitchen. "Hello, guys," Mr. Kelly said, "how ya doing?" We both were wearing masks of hospitality. "Fine," "Good," we said. "Well, it's great to see you both. You know what, guys?" Mr. Kelly leaned toward us, "I have a little something for you in the car. It's in a bag in the back seat. Go and check it out."

We were skeptical and excited at the same time as we rushed out the back door. I opened the door of the car and saw the bag from Andy's Sporting Goods with the handle of a bat sticking out. I reached in the car and got the bag — it was heavy. I set it down on the grass and we both looked in — baseball gloves, a ball, and the bat. I took out one glove and handed one to John. I held in my hand a catcher's mitt with Roy Campanella's name across the bottom, and John held an outfielder's glove with Carl Furillo's name written on the thumb. The Dodgers were our favorite team. Holding the gifts in our hands, we knew that these were very good gloves, maybe in the $40 dollar range. And we both kind of uttered "Wow" simultaneously.

In the kitchen I held the bag, John still held the Furillo glove. "Thank you, Mr. Kelly," John said, echoed almost immediately by me. "Well," Mr. Kelly said, "you did a great job. Thought you guys deserved something special for your work." I looked at my mother, and she had a smile on her face.

"I Think He's Dead"

One college summer, my brother and I worked at the Hot Shoppes in Cherrydale, Virginia. John worked the curb, running food orders out to cars, while I waited on tables inside. My brother-in-law Colin, in management for the Marriott Hotel Corporation, had secured us the jobs. My older brother Leo had bought us a 1956 orange and white Mercury, and so we had wheels. The last essential was a roof over our heads, and, even though money was tight, my sister Rose and Colin had welcomed us into their house for the summer, a small ranch house in Annandale; an invitation in retrospect that was pretty incredible — the house was small, without air-conditioning, and they had three children. Years later, she would talk about waking up late at night and hearing John and me counting our tips in the bedroom.

I had the night off and was home relaxing, probably watching television, when Danny, my chubby four-year old nephew, burst in through the screen door.

"Uncle Paul! Uncle Paul! Rhonda is making fun of me. She says she could beat me in a running race." (Rhonda was maybe 7 and the local bully among the kids on the block.)

"How can I help, Dan?"

Fidgeting he said, "Can I get on your shoulders, and we can race her together. Couldn't we, Uncle Paul?"

I wasn't thrilled about the idea, but I didn't like to see my favorite nephew made fun of, and so I said. "Let's do it, Dan."

On the sidewalk there were nine or ten kids milling around as we lined up for the race. Rhonda hadn't stopped, "Look at

Danny. Has to get his Uncle Paul to help him beat me. I don't care. I'll beat both of you." Danny adjusted his body. He definitely was a presence up there.

Some kid walked up and just said, "Go!" And we were off. I actually took the lead on the slow incline up the sidewalk past my sister's house. I could hear Rhonda thumping along just behind me. As I tried to accelerate, something went wrong, and I felt myself losing my balance. I tried to right my body, but Danny was too heavy; at first I was in slow motion and then the sidewalk rushed towards my face. We hit, my head a pillow for Danny's body. I felt him climbing off, and then looked up to see my sister walking at a good pace towards me, saying something like, "Oh dear, oh, dear."

She helped me get to my feet and then said, "Let's get inside and take care of this." My sister, a nurse, attended to my injuries, cleaning my face of sidewalk fragments. Abrasions across my forehead, the bridge of my nose, my cheekbones, my chin. After the cleaning and an antiseptic, she led me into the bedroom, and I stretched out on the bed. She returned shortly with some ice packs. As I lay there reflecting on the race and how Rhonda must have laughed to see our team go down — another victory for her — I heard voices outside the window. "I just saw him," one said, "I think he's dead."

I slept for a while and woke up at nearly eleven, I told my sister that I had to head in to pick up John at the Hot Shoppes. "You sure you're ok to drive?" she asked. "I'm fine, Rose, just my face."

I parked in a side lot at the Hot Shoppes but on the way in caught the attention of a few workers who were cleaning up the main car hop lot. Entering, I saw the night manager, Ray. "What the hell happened to you?"

"Had a little fall racing a neighborhood kid."

"What?" Ray was incredulous.

"It's all good. Street bully tried to humiliate my nephew in running, so we raced her together. Didn't make the finish line though."

'I see that."

"It's ok. I'm fine. I'll be in tomorrow night."

"Paul, you ain't working for at least a week with that face. I mean it. You think a customer wants to look at something like that?"

He was right, and so I had a week off to read and watch television and just relax. We never raced Rhonda again, but Danny got the last laugh. In raising his own three children, he told bedtimes stories about an awful girl named Rhonda who did terrible things at school, in stores, in her neighborhood, but she always got caught and always got in big trouble — every time. His message was, "Kids, don't ever be like Rhonda."

My First Car

Approaching midnight somewhere in northern New Jersey, I am driving on a long elevated structure, which could be a bridge or just an elevated highway, but I am pretty sure that the land I have risen above is an industrial wasteland, what a lot of people think of as northern New Jersey. I am just starting down a long stretch of highway when I see smoke coming from the front of my car. Not a good situation at all — not much space to pull over and tractor trailers barreling by every minute or so. I look at the dash — very simple panel in my Renault, nothing showing but then I see the problem. My emergency brake is on full — I can't believe it! I never disengaged the brake when I got back in my car after a coffee break over 30 miles back! With a few really good curses, I reach down and release the brake. Smoke seems to be a little thicker now — probably linked to my burnt out brake. The car is pretty much coasting, and I am tense watching these monster trucks approach out of the night behind me — they could run right over me in my little French car and not even be thrown off their track.

Hope appears suddenly when I see that the next exit is only one mile away — I am pretty much still coasting, the toll booth appearing in the distance. Now on the ramp I coast up to the booth.

The guy sees that my car is smoking and says, "You got a problem, bud."

"I know," I say, handing him my ticket. "Any gas stations still open?"

"Nah, but Rickie's Diner is about a quarter of a mile on the left. If you can make it there, you can use their phone."

"Thanks," I say, wondering if Rickie's Diner is where Perry and Dick stopped on their journey after leaving the Clutters.

I accelerate only slightly on the fairly level highway, thinking that maybe the brakes won't work at all by the time I get there. The sign for Rickie's Diner emerges out of the night. The diner itself is dimly lit, and there is one car in front of it. I coast in and shut my car off. Some smoke is still coming out of the front — maybe wheelbase, but at least it's not a flame. As I enter the diner, I smell the grease from a faded burger and see the cook leaning on the counter talking to a big guy in a dark shirt.

"Excuse me," I say. "Could I use your phone?"

"Yup," the cook says and points to his left where a phone rests on the wall. I look at my watch and see that it is almost 2 in the morning.

It's now 3:20 a.m., and I am in the back seat of a car being driven by one of my brother's good friends from college. The friend, whose name is also John, is giving me a hard time for forgetting to take the emergency brake off. "You owe me one, Paul, big time. Jesus, I had just gotten to sleep when your brother called and said that you were in trouble. Jesus. What a way to ruin a guy's night. Big time, Paul."

I smile and say sure, but what I am feeling is tremendous relief at being out of that situation and that world of steel and bridges and trailer trucks.

From my brother's fraternity house at college, I make arrangements to have the car towed to a local repair shop that some of my brother's friends have used over their time in college. The car will not be repaired for a few days, and so my brother and I get a ride home for Christmas break with his friend John, the same guy who rescued me. My brother has to return to the city two days after Christmas to go back to work at Hallmark Cards. He tells me that he will pick the car up.

A few days have passed, and I am at home sleeping when my mother's voice wakes me. "Yeah, Mom, what is it?" She shouts back, "It's the phone — your brother John. "

I stagger down the stairs in my pjs and enter the dining room where the phone sits next to my mother's rocking chair. I pick it up and sit down. "Hey," I say.

"Hey, I uh had a little problem last night," John says, in a voice that signals trouble.

"What happened?"

"Had a little situation with the car on the Long Island Expressway."

"You ok?" I ask.

"Yeah, just a little bruised up. Ahhhhh, I uhhh rolled the car over a couple of times — just missed getting hit by a tractor trailer."

"Jesus," I say. "Phew! Sure you're ok?"

"Yeah," he says, "I'm good. Car was in rough shape though. Had to be towed away."

"Ah, hey, what can you do? As long as you're not hurt. You back at Manhattan?"

"Yeah, State Police drove me back."

"Sure you're ok?"

"Yeah... Sorry about the car, Paul."

"It'll be fine," I say.

"Ok, I'll talk to you later. Police are going to let me know where the car was taken. I'll get someone to take me there and empty it out."

"Thanks, catch you later."

I put the phone down and sit in my Mom's chair, rocking slowly. I've had the car for five months, and now it is gone. The worst thing is that to save some money, I had taken the minimum of insurance, only extending coverage to myself as a driver. I know that for the next two years I will be paying on a car — $126 a month — that I don't have. After Christmas break, I will be back in D.C. catching the morning bus to graduate school.

Unexpected events and disappointing outcomes play a role in everyone's life. The key is in coming over time to see that such moments and events pale in significance to what really matters.

How I Got to Paris on a Catholic School Teacher's Salary

I had picked out my car, a maroon and white 1960 Mercury, one of its cool facets being a straight back window that I could control with a switch on the console. At the salesman's desk, I sat eager to wrap up the deal.

"Did you bring a check stub, Paul?"

"Sure," I said, reaching into my jacket pocket. I handed it across the desk to him.

He stared at it for a few seconds and then placed it on his desk. "Sorry, Paul, but I have to tell you that you don't make enough money to buy this car."

I was lost for words and muttered, "Really?"

He nodded and said, "Yeah, the only thing you can do is get someone to cosign it with you."

I thought of my brother Leo. "I can check tonight and let you know tomorrow," I said.

"Sure, sounds good. I know you like this car and want to get it."

"I do," I said.

Two days later, Leo and I sat across from my car salesman to wrap up the purchase of my car.

"Father, did you bring a check stub?"

"Sure," Leo reached into his coat pocket, pulled out a slip of paper, and handed it across the desk.

The salesman stared at the check stub. "Well, Father, your check stub says you make a salary of 4 thousand — and Paul makes a salary of 6 thousand." He paused and then smiled. "I guess between the two of you, you can buy the car."

One day later, I drove out of the dealership in my purple and white Mercury, a major smile on my face.

For three months the car would be my means of transportation from the apartment to school and around the Capital District. Then its life came to a sudden end on Exit 23 of the New York State Thruway.

My first few months teaching up to the Thanksgiving break were more difficult than I had ever imagined they would be. I loved Notre Dame High School and the people I worked with, but my own teaching was grinding along slowly — in brief, I could not keep up with the work that went into my classes. I had 5 classes and 5 preparations: one senior class, two junior classes — one Regents level, one not, and two sophomore classes — one Regents level, one not. Although the two junior classes and two sophomore classes had vocabulary and grammar books that were common in the grade level, each class had a different literature text and studied different paperbacks; for example, the sophomore Regents would study *The Scarlet Letter*, while the sophomore non-Regents would be reading *Mrs. Mike*. I was overwhelmed by the work and becoming more and more depressed. One rock to reach for and hold onto briefly in my dark waters was Thanksgiving break when I would have four-and-a-half days off.

After the Thanksgiving liturgy at school, I gathered my stuff and headed to Albany to pick up my brother who was a first-year student at Albany Med. I turned off the Thruway at Exit 23. The road turns and dips and then rises in a slow curve toward the exit booths. Half way up the rise, a jeep suddenly crossed the double yellow lines and headed right toward me. I remember hitting the brakes and trying to turn right, but the jeep was coming too fast and pretty much hit me head on. Neither vehicle had seat belts, and I remember seeing the passenger in the jeep hitting his head on the windshield and then bouncing backwards — his face almost instantly red.

The next hour or so is a blur in my mind, like the witnesses in Karl Shapiro's "Auto Wreck" with their sense of disorientation: Troopers in grey uniforms speaking quietly, an ambulance with doors open, red lights swirling, people walking around in slow motion, questions being asked, tow trucks. Then I recall a trooper driving me to my brother's apartment in Albany. My knee was hurting, and when I climbed the front steps of his flat, I felt that something might be wrong. When my brother arrived at the apartment from class, I asked him to check out my knee. After feeling the knee, he said, "You should be ok — it's probably just some bruising."

Back in school on Monday, my knee started a slow burn in the morning, and by afternoon when I tried to climb the stairs, the knee was in flames. In the school office, I reached my doctor in Troy, and he told me to go to St. Mary's Hospital and have an X-Ray. I am not quite sure how I managed to manipulate my right knee to drive my father's car, on loan for a few days, but somehow I made it to Troy.

The X-Ray showed a fractured patella, and a cast was placed on my leg an hour later. If teaching had been almost overwhelming up to Thanksgiving, now I would see how the inability to drive would make things a lot worse.

Each day, a priest who taught at the high school would pick me up at my apartment and then drive me home in the afternoon; occasionally inviting me to the rectory to have dinner with him and the pastor. But I was in deep water, and so on one Sunday night after family dinner a few weeks into December, it came out when I was being driven back to Schenectady by my brother. Near tears, I said, "I don't think I can do it, Leo. I can't keep up with the work. This teaching may not be for me."

The car was quiet. Then Leo spoke. "When I was first ordained, I was assigned to St. Paul's. You probably remember that the pastor there was Father Cronin, and he was a great mentor — he listened to me, and he guided me in the best way — giving me opportunities to try new things. But then in less than a year, he was transferred to Glens Falls. The next pastor had a lot of issues, and I was pretty much left on my own. Things were pretty rough at the rectory. But I was still excited about the priesthood and eager to fulfill my dreams. So I began trying some new things that were just being initiated in certain circles of the Church. I started saying the Mass facing the congregation — that seemed to make so much more sense to me. Nowadays we all do it, but then I was the rare bird. Well, I got a call from the Chancery — they had heard about what I was doing — and I was told to go back to the old way. This happened two or three more times with other innovations I tried, and I got pretty depressed — and even wondered about whether or not this vocation was the right one for me." His voice was calming and I was listening. "But I decided to ride out the rough waters and hang in there. In time I began to do some of the things I had been told I couldn't do, but now they were accepted. And I began to find more and more meaning in what I was doing. I began to see that the needs of people were great and that maybe I could make a difference. You know, Paul, I'm glad I stayed with the priesthood. You just might want to hang in for a while — things may begin to change."

When I got out of the car at my apartment, I felt a kind of peace and the element of hope. Over the next few months, Leo, even with his busy schedule, found time to come over and take me out to dinner, and most significant of all, he would show up right before my marks were due and help me organize my grading. I survived the year, and I was determined to make the coming summer one in which I would prepare myself well for a better second year.

Two weeks shy of two years after the car accident, a gentleman showed up at Notre Dame High School one

Keys on the Road

afternoon looking for me. I met him in the main hallway, and after he introduced himself and gave me his card, he said, "I'm from the insurance company of the two young men who were in the accident with you. I have a check for you from the insurance company for $200. If you will just sign it, all will be settled."

Something told me to be cautious. "I think I will wait until I talk with my brother," I said. "I'll get back to you in a couple of days."

That night I called Leo with the story. He listened and then said, "Call Bob Lynch in Scotia and see if he will take the case." I called Attorney Lynch, an old friend of Leo's, the next day, and he said, "Sure, I will take the case."

Over the next few months, I had to do paper work about the accident and visit St. Mary's to have my knee x-rayed — proof of the damage. And then one afternoon, Bob called and said, "Paul, would you settle for $2500. We could do more, but that is the initial offer." To me, $2500 was like a million dollars. I said, "Mr. Lynch, that is fine. I am very happy with the amount." Inside, I felt that I had just been visited by Michael Anthony of the television show "The Millionaire" and handed a check for one million dollars, tax free.

That spring I began to plan my visit to Paris.

And Then We Could See

My cousin Ray O'Brien was an inspiration. He had a way of making you feel that whatever you were doing was important, and he also had a great Irish sense of humor — reflected in both his natural laugh and understanding eyes. Ray was a long-time headmaster at St. Gregory's, a private elementary school in Loudonville, New York, and then head of development at LaSalle Institute, a private boys' high school in Troy. Ray's home in Troy was a welcoming center for friends, always charged with the spirit and joy of Ray, his wife Marian, and their nine children.

Michael, their first child, was born blind. I am sure that they must have grieved when they discovered this fact, but they were both strong people who fully accepted the challenges of life, and I never sensed that Michael was viewed as any less or treated differently than any of the other children. Ray and Marian had the ability to see each of their nine children as unique and special gifts of God. But it was Michael who taught me and many members of the O'Brien clan how to see.

For a number of years when I was growing up, our family would hold a picnic on land that had been the homestead of my mother — about 30 acres outside the village of Tomhannock. A few years after my brother had been ordained a priest, he was chatting with my parents one night and the subject of the old farm came up — the land with a stream running through it had been lying dormant. He asked them if my mother and her four brothers might be interested in selling it for a reasonable rate. I don't remember what the agreement was, but it was almost a gift to my brother. Then a house rose on the property due to the generosity of parishioners from my brother's parish. My father, now in retirement from the highway department, became the permanent caretaker.

The picnic took place on the lower portion of land, relatively flat, which was separated from the house by a stream. There was no car bridge yet across the stream, just a wooden walkway maybe three feet wide that traversed the 20 foot wide stream, which on this particular day was flowing well.

My father had gone over early in the day to finish his mowing and do some trimming. When we got there, a number of cousins were already into games and the grills were getting warmed up. As I sat at a table chatting with relatives, I noticed Michael navigating the grounds with his guide cane. I walked over to Ray, chatted for a moment, and then asked him if Michael would be safe on the unfamiliar terrain. Ray smiled and said, "Paul, don't worry about Michael, he will be fine."

And so the day passed — good food, laughter, stories galore, and games — until we decided with dusk approaching to go up to the house for what was an Irish tradition — sitting around my brother's piano and singing Irish songs. Music and laughter echoed in the night hills of Tomhannock. And then it was almost ten, and someone said, "Well, I suppose I should think of heading home." As we began to pack up our stuff, we heard the first person to step outside cry out, "Oh my God, it is pitch dark out here. Does anyone have a flashlight?" No one did, and as we stumbled down toward the stream, there was one thought foremost on our minds — how would we get across the water in the darkness?

When we reached the bank, we debated with nervous humor who would go first. Then we heard a voice from the other side. "It's easy — put your feet in the center of the foot bridge and walk directly to me. I will be at the center on this end. Just walk to my voice." And one by one we did. Michael, my blind cousin, had mastered the walk during the day and now was guiding those who could not see across the bridge in the evening's darkness.

At his father's funeral Mass, Michael offered the eulogy, which was written by Michael and his next oldest sibling, Joseph. At the close of the reflection, Michael said, "The best way to honor his life is to practice every day the kind of low key kindness that was so typical of Dad's way of doing things. It was because he paid attention; he really did care about all of us. We can leave the last word to poet George Santayana, who wrote, 'Calm was the sea to which your course you kept.'"

When I think about the darkness of the night and Michael's poise as he guided us across the water, I sense the calmness that reached through generations.

On the Edge: Scotch, Birds, Cell Phones, and Diners

Sometimes we underestimate others; sometimes teachers underestimate students. I know I did in the following case. The last class had ended on the half day before Christmas break, and I was gathering together the seasonal goodies on my desk — a box of homemade cookies, a few Christmas cards, and three presents from faculty members — when Matt walked into the room, holding a red and gold box marked J&B Scotch.

"Mr. O'Brien," Matt said, "just wanted to give you a little gift before leaving. You've been a good teacher." (Matt, a sophomore, was transferring to a large local suburban school.)

"That's very thoughtful, Matt. Just out of curiosity, how did you get this Scotch?"

"I asked my father to buy it for me so that I could give it to you. He made me put it in a brown bag and then carry it to school in a shopping bag."

"Amazing, well, thank you, Matt, and thank your Pop too. I will miss you in class, especially your sense of humor."

"We'll keep in touch, Mr. O'Brien, and, listen, enjoy that Scotch."

I am not much of a Scotch whiskey type of drinker, so after telling Debbie about the gift, I put the Scotch away behind our small wine rack.

Early Sunday afternoon a few months later, we were awaiting the arrival of my brother Leo and my mother who were coming for Easter dinner. As usual, Debbie and I were in a bit of a frenzy trying to get everything ready, and it was getting close to two p.m., their arrival time.

"When they get settled," Debbie said, "see if they would like something to drink — we have red and white wine. And soda."

"Sure." And then I remembered. "Hey, Leo likes Scotch. I'll get Matt's J&B out and have it ready."

I reached behind the wine rack and grabbed the Christmas gift. When I opened the box, I looked twice. Inside was a bottle with a dark liquid and wrapped around the bottle was a magazine. I lifted the bottle up and saw that it was a "Bully Hill" red. Then I reached for the magazine — "Hustler!"

A big smile crossed my face, and at the same time, I was so relieved that I had not opened this thoughtful Christmas gift in front of my brother and mother.

When I returned to school, I told a couple of Matt's friends to tell him that I had opened his Christmas gift on Easter Sunday and that I appreciated his thoughtful and generous gift.

I liked Josh. He was one of these kids that can seemingly do no wrong because he is so likable: outgoing, easy smile, lots of good friends — always with the little quip or thought that makes teachers smile. His dream was to be a successful businessman, and his favorite television show was *The Apprentice*. He wanted to get on the show and display his ingeniousness and cleverness to Donald Trump. He even carried in his wallet a dollar signed by the Donald, whom he had met one summer at Saratoga Race Track.

This particular day as I recall was in the early fall, and I believe the class was the period right before lunch. We were doing *A Streetcar Named Desire*, and the play as always had enough power and attraction to hold the class. In my classroom the students faced the blackboard, and the windows and street were behind them. Into the frames of my windows pulled a car, riding partly up on the sidewalk. Three young men got out, dressed in jeans and sweatshirts, and stood facing the school. "Hey, Gibbons," they yelled. "Eat this!" By now, my class had turned to the window and saw the three students holding up their middle fingers. Before I could say anything, Josh, who was seated in the fourth seat in the third row, got up, went to the window, pulled it more completely open, and put his right arm out the window, with his own bird prominently rising into the air, "Back at ya," he said.

"Josh, get away from that window!" I said. The class was loving his response to the street students. "That's totally inappropriate! I am going to have to give you a detention for that little action." By now the three outsiders (the local public high school had had the day off) had climbed back into their car and were gone. Josh looked at me with his inimitable smile and said, "Mr. O'Brien, I probably deserve that one."

As he sat down, I secretly wanted to applaud what he did, but I could not because proper and correct behavior meant that one does not replicate the crude and inappropriate behavior of others. To this day, I still smile when I think of that moment.

It might have been a Friday night when the call took place. I had stopped briefly at Walgreens to buy a couple of items, and then I was heading to pick up Agnes, my mother-in-law, and take her to Petta's Restaurant where the family was gathering. Everyone in the family had been pretty busy at their work sites, and it was no problem for me to stop and give her a lift. I did realize though that I was running a little late. And so as I waited at the red light, I thought I should give her a quick call and let her know I was running late.

The phone started ringing.

The light changed, and as I was turning left onto Central Avenue, a dark, sports car barreled through the red light just missing me by inches. I exploded with a combination of words that were pure adrenaline, "You mother-f_ _ _ ing, c _ _ _ sucking, son of a bitch, you g _ _ - d _ _ _, f _ _ _ _ _ _ douche bag," and the words poured out until — THE PHONE! I hit the word "End" on my phone.

I waited about two minutes and then pulled over near a car wash and called again.

"Hello, Agnes," I said in the softest tone I could muster.

"Oh my God!" she blurted out. "I can't tell you — I, I just had the most horrible call — oh dear, goodness, I dont' know!"

"Really?" I said, again in a soft tone.

"The crudest words I have ever heard — I can't even repeat them — they were so horrible, oh it was just awful."

"Listen, you will be fine. Probably some idiot who was angry at a friend, missed the number he was calling, and got you by mistake."

"No one should be talking like that — it wasn't even human — just horrible."

"You'll be fine," I said, calmly. I should be there in about five minutes.

I quickly called my wife and told her what had happened. "I can't explain except to say that the guy who ran the light nearly killed me, and I just lost it."

"She'll be ok, after a while. That is pretty funny. And she didn't make any connection with you?"

"No, I was screaming the obscenities into the phone, but when I called her I was really calm and soft-spoken. Got to go, Henry's calling."

Debbie's brother had called to see what time we were meeting for dinner. I told him and then told him what had just happened. "Oh gees," he said, "why did you do that?"

"I didn't do it on purpose, Hen, it was just bad timing."

"Jeepers," he said. "Hope Aggie will be ok — awful thing to do to her."

Shortly after we were seated, Agnes brought up the horrible phone call. Debbie and Henry were appropriately attentive as she painfully recounted the incident, and they joined the chorus of family members who were sympathetic, all in agreement that it must have been some idiot who had gotten the wrong number or something like that. I breathed a sigh of relief.

In time the rest of the siblings heard about who the caller was; at first, a sense of disbelief, then a lot of laughs at the incongruity of it all. And whenever, usually at Sunday breakfast with the family, Agnes would bring up the horrible phone call she once got, the family would shake their head sideways in support of her and then glance my way, and, if Agnes wasn't looking at them, give me a smile. Agnes never found out that her son-in-law was that horrible caller.

Thank God.

We arrived at the Palace Diner about 11 p.m. — the place was very quiet, just the three of us and two women in a booth. I had told Mom that it would probably be about mid-night when we got home. With the concert running until about 9 or so, followed by some socializing and then having to drive Ron back to South Troy, it would take some time. She said, "I will leave the shrine light on for you." In our back yard was a small shrine to the Blessed Virgin. In the ceiling of the shrine's roof, an electrician had placed a light, which, much to our consternation, was visible from my parents' bedroom. The light switch was on the back porch. When the light went out, we were home. My guess is that my mother woke up often to check the light. We used to try to think of ways we could shut it off with a small remote at some distance, but we were never able to come up with a solution.

It had been a fun evening, my brother John, friend Ron, and I playing maybe twenty or so folk songs from that time period — Clancy Brothers, Kingston Trio, The Weavers. Our audience was my brother's youth group — he was a priest stationed at St. Paul's in Schenectady — in the gym of the school. Some of the songs were sing-a-longs, and that made the evening even more enjoyable. So when we sat down at the counter of the Palace Diner, we felt pretty happy and a bit hungry. I can't remember what we ate — probably burgers and fries, but at one point the counter man, who I think was also the owner, said, "What are you guys doing out tonight?" And we told him about the concert in Schenectady. "Sounds good," he said. "You got your guitars with you?" We nodded, and he said, "Bring 'em in — let's hear a few tunes."

We did and cranked out a few of our favorites, "Tom Dooley" being at the top of the list. While we were playing, the two women got into it, joining in the singing. When we were done, one of them said, "That was a lot of fun — you guys are pretty good."

My brother set his guitar down and moved into the booth with one of the women; I did the same on the other side, Ron still on a stool at the counter. Two women in their mid-30's; three high school boys, 17 and 18 years old.

At one point — I was not Ernest Hemingway — I asked the women, "What do you two do for a living?" I felt a direct kick under the table to my shin from my brother and looked at him, realizing the dumbness of my question. One of the women smiled and said, "We're in business for ourselves." I probably said, "Ok," or something , and the conversation then went on with my brother in the lead.

At one point, the woman next to me looked at her watch, "Well, it's after one — we should think about going." Like true gentlemen, my brother and I slid out and stood back so that the two women could exit gracefully.

We payed our bill right after the women and said our good-byes. As we watched them get into their car, parked down the street a bit, I turned to John and Ron and said, "Let's follow them."

They headed down into the heart of Troy, cruising slowly. I was thinking how in movies the car following is always too close and too obvious, but with the very thin traffic, it was no problem staying back, provided that one navigated the stop and go lights well. They turned right on Fifth Avenue and drove toward North Troy. When they reached Hoosick Street, they took a left and headed toward the Hudson River. At the bottom of Hoosick, they took a right onto River Street, and continued driving for another four or five blocks, then pulled over and parked, a couple of car lengths from a bar. We pulled in about half a block away and doused the headlights. The women got out and walked toward the bar. They turned right at a staircase and began to climb it, heading for what seemed to be an apartment located above the bar. They reached the landing and entered the apartment.

We sat there, and Ron said, "Well, that's that." I said, "Wait — Ron, see if you can find a piece of paper back there, something I can write a note on. John, check the glove compartment for a pencil." Ron found a piece of lunch bag paper and handed it to me. John found a pen.

I wrote a note, folded it, and got out of the car. I ran to where they had parked, lifted up the windshield wiper, and placed the note there. As I got back to our car, my brother said, "What did the note say?"

"If you really want to see Troy, call this number" — our home number — "at noon tomorrow."

"You serious?" John said.

"Holy Crap," Ron added.

We had to drive Ron back to South Troy and then drive out to our home in Raymertown, a good distance from Ron's. It was after three when we pulled into the driveway at home. The light was still on over the Blessed Virgin. In the small outdoor porch, I gently moved the switch to off, hoping beyond hope that my mother had fallen into a mini-Rip Van Winkle snooze.

Dad was seated at the kitchen table sipping some tea, yesterday's newspaper in front of him. "Hello, boys," he said.

"Hi, Dad, " I said, "little late, but no problems."

"Good to hear," he said and took a sip of tea.

The door to the dining room, which had been closed, flew open and my mother stood there in her housecoat, hair wild. Not a Medusa image quite, but close. "Where in God's name have you been?" she demanded.

I took the lead, "We got a little hung up, chatted for quite a while at St. Paul's, then stopped at the Palace Diner in Troy — the owner actually asked us to bring our guitars in and play.

There were a few people there, and they liked our music, so we played for a while."

"Well, this is so wrong, getting in at this hour." My mother was a firm believer that the later the night got, the more likely there would be trouble. I would have agreed with her in this situation. "The two of you — get up to bed — this is just awful."

"I turned Mary's light off," I said.

"That light should have been off a lot earlier. Just awful, "she said.

The phone was ringing, and I looked at the clock in my bedroom. It was exactly noon. "Oh God!" I said. And then my mother's voice at the foot of the stairs. "Paul, it's for you."

I was doomed. We had only one phone in our house, and it was on a stand in the living room, only a few feet from the kitchen, my mother's command center. How could I dodge this bullet? The phone seemed to rush towards me as I entered the dining room as if to say, "Got you now, Smart-ass."

I picked it up and in a weak voice said, "Hello."

"Paul, it's Leo. You left your jacket here last night." I gave a huge sigh of relief.

I knew I had to keep Leo on the line for at least ten minutes — kill her call period. And so we talked about the concert, the music, and the kids in his youth group. After some time had elapsed, I said, "John and I will cruise over — maybe tomorrow — and grab the jacket."

I had survived but was left with one nightmarish thought: What could I have shown about Troy to a Lady of the Night?

Roger and JFK

When Sully said, "I have a couple of complementary tickets for the Army-Navy game next month in Philadelphia, want to go?" I said sure. Traveling with Sully to a football game had an excitement all its own. A month earlier he had taken me to a Jets game. We were running a bit late, and I had asked him where he was going to park since there didn't seem to be a spot for miles. He said, "Got it covered." And within minutes we pulled up to a gate guarded by security police. One approached the car, and Don took out of his jacket a badge, held it to the window, and said, "Sullivan, security." A quick glance, and the policeman stepped back, signaled to have the gate opened, and we drove in.

I asked him what that was all about, and he said, "My father was a detective with the City police. It's his badge, works every time." In our post 9/11 world, I don't think that we would have gotten by security so easily.

Sitting in Philadelphia Stadium on that late fall day, I remember looking around and thinking that the number of people present was more than the entire city of Troy, the closest city to my home village of Raymertown. Our seats were very good, complementary tickets to the Sullivan family, at about the forty-five yard line. The sun was shining, and it seemed almost like a summer day, at least in my memory.

I had never seen anyone like the Navy quarterback, a young guy by the name of Roger Staubach. Tall, elusive, with pinpoint passing, he thrilled the crowd, at least all those who were Navy fans. He danced, dodged, ducked, wove by, through, and around tacklers. Pure magic. And from where we sat, we looked directly across the field at the celebrating Midshipmen in blue and gold. In front of the contingent sat President John Kennedy. I remember thinking that this was a pretty special day.

At half-time, President Kennedy, accompanied by the Secret Service, crossed the field and took a seat somewhere near the 50-yard line. As I recall, he seemed to be a few rows up from ours. And now it was a glorious struggle for me — to choose my focus. Between the young dazzling quarterback of Navy, or the man who had become a hero in our household, a modern Arthur who had ventured out from Camelot to see young heroes engaged in sport. At one point, I remember that a light gust of wind had blown the back of his hair up — and the color was auburn, at least that's how it appeared in the afternoon sun.

Navy won that day, and I remember thinking on the way back to New Rochelle that I had been part of a special moment. Less than a year later on North Avenue in New Rochelle, I heard on a car radio that President Kennedy had been shot. Shortly after that, he was dead.

To see him celebrating and full of life at a great sports' event in Philadelphia and then to hear on a car radio that in some distant city he had been assassinated — this was one of the hardest eclipses life had presented.

But I would see Roger Staubach again, up close and personal. I was working as a waiter at the Twin Bridge Marriott, while attending graduate school at Catholic University. One afternoon, we were called together by our restaurant manager and told that Roger Staubach would be spending the first night of his honeymoon in our hotel, and he would be having breakfast with us the following morning. "Because you are all excellent waiters, we will draw straws to see who gets to wait on Mr. Staubach." I can't remember exactly how many of us were on the morning/lunch shift — maybe twelve — but I think we all wanted the opportunity with this customer. I won the draw.

He was the coolest person I ever waited on — oh, his wife was pretty, but I was waiting on the dashing and daring Roger Staubach, the incredible quarterback from Navy. I can't remember what he had with his eggs —I do remember coffee — but I will never forget how nervous I was when I asked him if I could have his autograph. He smiled and said, "Sure," and I placed a piece of paper and a pen next to him. I almost sensed his wife shudder a bit — as if to say, well here we go — but it may have been my imagination. For me, his presence and his signature were the perfect close to my personal introduction to Roger Staubach.

When Roger was drafted by the Dallas Cowboys after completing his duties as a naval officer, I was a loyal fan of the New York Giants. Yet, in the years to come he always left me with a sense of his special grace, a notch or two above the rest, even when the Cowboys beat my Giants.

"Something bigger was going on here."

Tom Verducci - "Nine Innings from Ground Zero"

Jimmy Valvano had been head basketball coach at my Alma Mater, Iona College, from 1975 until 1980, the biggest win under Valvano a February 1980 upset of second-ranked Louisville 77- 60 at Madison Square Garden. That spring Louisville won the National Championship. Two months after that win, Valvano accepted the position of head basketball coach at North Carolina State. I remember at the time feeling a little anger toward Valvano and a sense of loss for Iona, even though all good coaches at small colleges get offers to move on. I had an outlet for my feelings, however, because at that time I was also a big fan of the North Carolina Tar Heels. I had read a lengthy profile of Dean Smith in a sports magazine and had begun to follow the team. Now I could back a team that could beat Valvano's.

It was in 1981, the year after Valvano's arrival at NC State, that Michael Jordan accepted a scholarship to North Carolina. In his freshman year, the Tar Heels won the 1982 National Championship. The following year, however, the Tar Heels were defeated in the ACC Tournament by Valvano's Wolfpack, the second win in a miraculous and dazzling nine straight wins as the Wolfpack won the 1983 National Championship. My allegiance shifted to the Wolfpack in the Championship game when they faced the seemingly invincible and dominant Houston Cougars.

In a game that would in time become etched forever in my mind, the Wolfpack won on a shot by Lorenzo Charles who grabbed an attempt by Dereck Whittenburg that fell short, and Charles jammed it through the hoop at the buzzer for the win.

That win was the high point in Jim Valvano's basketball career as a coach, but he would have one higher point: receiving the 1993 ESPN Arthur Ashe Courage Award. His body filled with cancer, Coach Valvano stood at the podium knowing that his time was drawing to a close and that on this occasion he could do something for others. He spoke about his life, his beliefs, and his hopes. His words speak simply and eloquently: *"Time is very precious to me. I don't know how much I have left, and I have some things I would like to say.... When people say to me how do you get through life or each day, it's the same thing. To me there are three things we should do every day of our lives. Number one is laugh. You should laugh every day. Number two is think. You should spend some time in thought. Number three is you should have your emotions moved to tears, could be happiness or joy. But think about it. If you laugh, you think and you cry, that's a full day. That's a heck of a day. You do that seven days a week, you're going to have something special.... I urge all of you, all of you, to enjoy your life, the precious moments you have.... with ESPN's support, which means what? Their money and their dollars and their helping me — we are starting the Jimmy V Foundation for Cancer Research. And its motto is, 'Don't give up...don't ever give up.' And that's what I'm going to try to do every minute that I have left.... I know. I gotta go. I gotta go; and I got one last thing, and I said it before, and I'm gonna say it again. Cancer can take away all my physical abilities. It cannot touch my mind, it cannot touch my heart, and it cannot touch my soul. And those three things are going to carry on forever. I thank you, and God bless you all."*

Sometimes television can help us to see more clearly and feel more deeply. In May, 2013, ESPN's "30 for 30" presented "Survive and Advance," the story of North Carolina State and their unbelievable run to the National Championship. The documentary begins with star guard Dereck Whittenburg on his way to gather with his fellow players and coaches on the 30th anniversary of the Championship. The question he asks in the opening of the documentary: what was the meaning in the story of their victory run and of the Coach who inspired them?

Thurl Bailey, forward on the Wolfpack team, said that he discovered on the journey that the 1983 team taught him hope, the idea of never ever quitting, and the idea that if you never stop believing and loving each other, "You can accomplish miracles." Bailey captured the idea with a letter Coach Valvano had read to the team from a lady whose husband was in a coma. The husband was a basketball fan, she wasn't, but in the hospital room, she would turn the game on because maybe he could hear it. And then she began following the team as they started their run of incredible wins and wrote, "You guys have given me a reason to believe." Bailey was taken back with the realization that "we were representing something we couldn't even fathom before; this is not just about us winning games, this is about hope."

Near the end of the documentary there is a scene when the team returns to the University on the Tenth Anniversary of the Championship - they were not sure that Coach Valvano, very sick with cancer, would make it. He did, and he hugged each player. Thurl Bailey: "It was hard for me, that's not the way I wanted to remember him. He came up and I helped him up on the chair. He put his arms around me and in my ear, said, 'I love you.' And I said, 'I love you too, Coach.'"

In his brief words that day, Coach Valvano said, "Lastly, what this team taught me is to love each other and we don't talk enough about this in sports.... When you have a dream and you throw in that concept of never stop believing in and loving each other, you can accomplish miracles, and that's what the 83 team taught me."

"Survive and Advance" closes with the words of Jim Valvano's wife, Pam. Her husband always kept note cards with his dreams on the cards in his sports jackets — phrases like

"Win the National Championship"; the last card she took out of his jacket said, "Beat Cancer."

"Survive and Advance" showed us the miraculous journey of North Carolina State in winning the 1983 college basketball championship, but it also showed us the great sadness the team and community experienced in seeing their beloved coach battle against and eventually succumb to cancer. Yet in his words after receiving the ESPN Arthur Ashe Courage Award, Jimmy Valvano rose to heroic heights and gave the speech of his lifetime inspiring others to continue the great battle against cancer.

Where does one find the strength to go on? After the tragedy of September 11, 2001, the people of New York City were in a state of shock and grief, along with much of the Nation. "The worst day in the history of the City," said Mayor Giuliani. For many, the sport of baseball became a kind of balm, a relief, something they could lose themselves in for a night. "Nine Innings from Ground Zero," an HBO special, tells the story of how baseball, especially three World Series games in the Bronx between the New York Yankees and the Arizona Diamondbacks, served to lift the spirits of those who had suffered loss in the attack on the Twin Towers.

Twelve year old Brielle Saraceni had lost her father, the Captain of Flight 195 that hit the South Tower. In her long period of silence, she wrote a letter to Derek Jeter, her favorite player, about her loss. Shortly after the writing, Derek called and invited her up to Yankee Stadium. Ellen Saraceni, her mom, said that after the telephone call from Derek Jeter, Brielle went up to her room and started singing, the first time she had heard her sing since 9/11. A few days later, Brielle and her mom met Derek at the Stadium, a thrilling occasion for her. Looking back at that moment, Brielle said, "Baseball just made 9/11 a little better for us."

In the ninth inning of Game 4, Tino Martinez hit a two-out, two-run homer to tie the score 3-3. And in the tenth, with two outs, Derek Jeter stepped to the plate and hit a two-out homer for the Yankee win, 3-2. Tom Verducci offers a thought about the night: "You think about the raw emotion that everybody took to the ballpark that night, and you begin to think that something bigger is going on here, and we just have to sit back and watch it play out."

Kieran Lynch's two brothers died in the North Tower. Kieran, Sean, and Farall had been loyal Yankee fans, but after the tragedy, Kieran struggled to carry on without his brothers. His first trip back to Yankee Stadium was Game 5 of the World Series. "Stepping into Yankee Stadium for the first time after 9/11 was a connection to my brothers. I felt I had to be at the game." In the bottom of the 9th inning, with two outs and the Yankees losing 2 to 0, Scott Brosius hit a two-run tying homer. Kieran said that he started high-fiving those around him and even hugging complete strangers. "I had never been part of anything like that in my life." In Games 4 and 5, the Yankees had come back to win in dramatic fashion. "Those two games lifted the spirits of New York," said Mayor Giuliani, "and the Yankees had the city on their shoulders."

All who follow sports know that the Yankees did not win the Series, even though Curt Schilling of the Diamondbacks was convinced that he had lost Game Seven. With the Yankees up 2 to 1, Schilling was pulled from the game after giving up a home run to Alfonso Soriano. "I gave up the home run that cost us the game. They've got Mariano Rivera in the bullpen, so the game is over." It wasn't. Arizona defeated the New York Yankees as Rivera faltered and the Diamondbacks rallied.

Scott Brosius said, "Life is not fair. If there was ever a fair time for the Yankees to win the World Series, that was the year." The City had suffered a terrible loss, and the Yankees with their great closer also had lost.

Still, as the documentary shows, baseball, that pure and simple sport, had served as a form of healing for many. Joined together, people had found relief, and their spirits had been lifted in "the simple joy" of watching a baseball game.

Big Apple

A birthday present to me. Saturday in New York at Christmastime. My wife had proposed it a week earlier. Amtrak, a walk to the Morgan Library to see the Charles Dickens' manuscript of "A Christmas Carol," a taxi up to the Metropolitan Museum of Art's Angel Tree, lunch somewhere (we were counting on serendipity), St. Patrick's Cathedral and the shrine of Bishop John Neumann, Rockefeller Center, the Tree, the ice skaters, a visit to the Gotham Book Mart, and home on the train. A full day. The sun was shining as we awoke.

Though the train was very crowded, we found seats right behind two friends from Albany, a mother and daughter who were also celebrating Christmas in the city. Having stocked up on our own goodies — sliced oranges and buttered hard rolls — I walked to the cafe car for coffee and tea. And then we were set. Deborah was well into Philip Pullman's *The Amber Spyglass*, and I had my stack of newspapers — *Daily Gazette*, *Times Union*, *New York Post*, and *New York Times*. The train was cosy, the food was tasty, and the news was overflowing — Gore, Bush, and all the Friday night sports. After I finished each paper, I passed it on to our friends in front of us.

And we were there. On our walk to the Morgan Library, the wind nipped at our faces, but the sun more than balanced the brisk air. I was lucky because the Morgan Library's fall exhibit was on John Ruskin. I had studied Ruskin briefly in college years ago, but I had never seen his drawings, sketchbooks, original manuscripts, including both scholarly architectural commentary and literary criticism, as well as some incredibly moving letters and notes, the most painful being a scribbled page as Ruskin was descending into madness in his old age.

The Dickens' manuscript was in a study that also included wonderful first editions such as *The Adventures of Huckleberry Finn*, Darwin's *Origin of Species*, and original handwritten works by Bach, Beethoven, and Mozart. But the Dickens' manuscript had a special power — maybe it was the season. I spent most of the precious time in the study looking at the master's original work — so human with cross-outs, word changes, new words squeezed in above and along the side. This is it, I thought. A work in progress. A master's work in progress. And next to the messy manuscript, a small book of the final text. So pure and clean.

Serendipity was present. The small courtyard of the Morgan was a dining room, naturally lit by a glass roof and softened by an ivied wall and indoor trees. We ordered. Soup, sandwiches, quiche, and a glass of wine. Perfect.

Then we were being whipped through the city by a taxi driver who told us he had gotten stuck earlier in the day for four hours at the airport. Cutting in and out, weaving, zigging and zagging, narrowly missing other cars. And there it was — the Metropolitan Museum of Art.

What a crowd! Security inside the front door ushered the visitors along to avoid gridlock. We had a destination: the Angel Tree. Decorated with a multitude of angels, the tree dominated the Museum's Medieval Sculpture Hall. What really took one's breath away were the scores of handmade figures, both human and animal, that stood in awe of or moved by instinct toward the moment of nativity. Deborah pointed out her favorite figure, a dark-skinned man, simply dressed, carrying a heavy load on his back.

Then we separated for a time, she to explore some medieval art, I to spend a little time at the modern art exhibit, where I was delighted to discover a painting I had seen often in books — Picasso's "Gertrude Stein." A ponderous presence celebrated in earth tones and radiating power and thought.

Keys on the Road

I have never experienced a driver so exasperated by traffic as our cab driver on the way to St. Patrick's Cathedral. Twice I felt the impact of bumpers from other cars. Though we were almost in gridlock, he refused to acknowledge it and kept crossing lines at 45 degree angles to edge ahead a car length or two.

St. Patrick's. We expected a crowd but not nearly the packed church we found. Monitors along the side aisles showed Cardinal Egan speaking at a special celebration of the Hawthorne Dominican Sisters. We squeezed through the crowd to the shrine of Bishop John Neumann, always an oasis for us when visiting New York. The white stone sculpture radiates peace, compassion, and understanding. The bishop sits quietly; close to him a young boy and a young girl read from a book. We made an offering, lit a candle, and said a prayer.

Outside, a young couple were arguing about whether or not to bring their baby carriage into the cathedral. He kept saying, "No way," and she kept asking why? We smiled. He was right. There was no way a baby carriage could navigate inside.

The Rockefeller Center Christmas Tree beckoned, but I had a more personal goal. The ice rink. Never have I thought about the rink or looked at it without thinking of *The Catcher in the Rye* and Holden Caulfield. I scanned the rink for Holden's Sally Hayes, and there she was. A young, attractive high school girl, skated backwards and then turned into a spin, narrowly missing the clumsy skaters who lurched past her. She came down, offered us all a smile, and skated off. Ah yes, Holden, you were right.

On the way to Times Square, we turned down 47th Street and stepped into the Gotham Book Mart. We browsed for a while, I bought a small copy of Dylan Thomas's "A Child's Christmas in Wales," and while paying heard a customer say, "This is still the best bookstore in the city," and then we were back out onto the bustling street.

It was starting to get a bit late, and the crowded street made movement slow. My wife suggested we take the subway from Times Square to Penn Station. Though I always feel as if I'm descending into a lonely cave in the New York Subway, this was a good time because the platform was crowded with cheerful people, many seemingly touched by the spirit of Christmas.

Climbing the stairs to the Amtrak Station, I saw a figure covered by a long blanket on a kind of flat platform under the stairs. As we got closer, I could see that the blanket was a tattered afghan. Long and dirty, the faded yellow and brown afghan reached from the person's feet to his head. I could see now that his body rested on flattened cardboard boxes. I couldn't see any movement, any sign of breathing, and then we disappeared up to the next level.

Riding home on the train, I held a book in my hand, but I was thinking about the day, this present to me: Dickens and Ruskin and the Morgan Library, the quiet, elegant setting for lunch, the mad race to the Met., the Angel Tree, Gertrude Stein, St. Patrick's and Bishop Neumann, the Rockefeller Tree, the rink and Holden, the Gotham Book Mart, and the subway, culminating in the image of the man with the afghan.

More than thirty years ago, my mother gave me an afghan as a birthday present, and over the years, she made one for each of her children and then all of her grandchildren. The one she gave me rests on our bed, a comfort and a blessing during afternoon naps and late in the night when the room becomes chilled. A blessing. And I thought of the journey of the man or woman who seemed to have nothing but the afghan. And then I said a prayer.

Back to Class

What was playing in my mind when I looked at the stage was Thomas Wolfe's story "The Far and the Near," where at the end of the story the narrator's mind is one of disorientation and disillusion. The theater was so small. My last memory of a stage production in Doorley Hall was Harold Pinter's "The Caretaker," when I was a junior in college. That night, the upstairs theater was packed with students who roared at the dialogue for much of the play and then became quite subdued as Harold Pinter's darker, absurdist side took over in the second act.

Tonight the stage extended far out into the room, and only two rows of chairs were placed on the sides and directly in front of the stage, room enough for about 40 people. The production was Neil Simon's "The Star Spangled Girl."

I had traveled down to Iona College with colleagues from Notre Dame-Bishop Gibbons to participate in a four-day workshop dedicated to articulating the essential elements of a Christian Brother education. Our little group had seen on the bulletin board in our dorm that the theater festival was taking place, and tonight was "The Star Spangled Girl."

At intermission, I descended into the basement to buy a soda and then walked up to the first floor, where many of my classes were held when I was a student in the 60's. Ahead of me in the hallway, a man dressed in a dark sport jacket seemed to be looking around for something. "Can I help you?" I asked. The man turned toward me and said, "No, I'm fine. I know my away around here."

His voice was more revealing than his face — a rich bass instrument one couldn't forget. "Mr. Chetta," I said, "Paul O'Brien, class of 1965. I had you for two classes in English." He smiled and reached out to shake my hand. When I told him that I was teaching English at a Brothers' school upstate, he smiled, and then told me that Iona had just recognized him at graduation for his 40 years of service to the school.

At Iona, Mr. Chetta had taught me a lesson about not taking short-cuts. In his modern novel course, we were expected to read a novel a week, and for each novel we were to write a two-page reaction paper. As *The Grapes of Wrath* loomed before me, I decided that I would seek out some aid for my reflection. In the library, I found an essay about the novel, read it, and then wrote my reaction to *Grapes of Wrath* without ever citing the critical source. A few days later, Mr. Chetta returned the paper with an F at the bottom and the comment, "I can read essays too. Do your own work."

Earlier that day, I had pointed out to a colleague the exact spot on North Avenue — almost in front of the college — where I had heard the tragic news. On my way to Mr. Chetta's 1 p.m. American Lit class, cars were abruptly pulling over into parking spaces. I could hear voices from car radios. "Anything wrong?" I asked one driver who had pulled up near me. "The President's been shot. Looks pretty bad, they say." In front of the classroom, Mr. Chetta told us that there would be no class. "Do what you need to do." In the quad, about 200 Iona students started to recite the Rosary. I joined them.

As the audience filed out of "The Star-Spangled Girl," Mr. Chetta walked over to me to say good-bye. After telling him how great it was to see him again, I asked him if the Beechmont was still a place we as adults could get a bite to eat. When I was a student at Iona, the Beechmont on North Avenue, a stone's throw from the college, was the number one watering hole for the students. "Oh sure," he said, "they even have menus now with a pretty good selection."

We made our way through the bar area, pretty crowded with young people, into the back dining area, which had one empty booth. We had just ordered drinks and some nachos when our past returned.

"Oh my God, it is you guys! I couldn't believe it when you walked past us in the bar!" Standing in front of us was Kelly, a former student at the high school whom we had all taught. I am not sure she realized how much her wide-eyed look conveyed. Her old high school teachers were on her turf, in her world. "I can't believe it! What are you doing here?"

For the next hour, we shared stories and memories of students past and present. A graduate of Iona College a few years prior, Kelly was now working for a business firm in New York City and living in New Rochelle. Her life had come together very well. Before we departed, she promised to visit the high school in the fall and talk about the experience of college and what one needs to do to navigate the difficult waters.

The next day, when we had a break in the conference, I walked into Doorley Hall and entered the classroom where I had taken a course from Mr. Chetta. I sat down in the third row, two seats back, my favorite seat. The room was very still, and I could feel the thread of life weaving the past, the present, and the future together. I was closing in on forty years of teaching myself. There was something good about being close to the source and an inspiration.

Roots

In 1968, when my parents traveled to Ireland, my mother kept a journal. It began, "So now through the great goodness of God, we are starting our trip to Ireland — a nice, warm feeling to visit the land from which our ancestors sailed so many, many years ago. The O'Briens sailed from County Waterford to settle in Pittstown, and the Madigans from Limerick to settle in Tomhannock. How hard they all worked to raise their children to be good and decent citizens, and especially to keep the faith in living their lives. They did well, so well, these old folks."

With these words etched in my mind, my wife and I arrived in Ireland, and my heart leapt up when an elderly Christian Brother, after hearing my name, said, "Welcome home."

For over 40 years, I had known of the work of the Christian Brothers in Schenectady, and for many years, I had taught with the Brothers at Notre Dame-Bishop Gibbons School. Now I stood on the grounds of the first school established by Blessed Edmund Ignatius Rice, the founder of the Christian Brothers in Ireland.

In 1802, at his school at Mt. Sion, Waterford, Edmund Rice had reached out to feed, clothe, and educate the poor youth of Ireland. And for three days, Brother Barney, Brother Frank, and seven other Christian Brothers made their home at Mt. Sion a warm and hospitable setting for our small group of travelers — Brother Kevin, Brother Joe, my wife Deborah and me. They shared with us their knowledge of Edmund Rice, their stories of Ireland, their Irish humor, and their home-cooked meals. I was growing in an awareness that, "Yes, you can go home again."

We had received an offer of a Kilkenny countryside tour and dinner from Father Jim Hayes, born in Ireland, and then serving as prison chaplain at Great Meadow Correctional Facility in New York. He was back in Ireland visiting his family and, on a sunny Saturday afternoon, he met us at Duiske Abbey, Graignamanagh. In the quiet coolness of the church, Father Hayes spoke of his own childhood, his family attending this very church for weekly Mass, his Confirmation, and the Mass he celebrated at a side altar for his mother's and her twin sister's 90th birthday.

Then he led us by car into the countryside of Ireland and, after a few miles, pulled over near a small ruin. A sign the shape of an arrow read, "Saint Moling's Well." We followed Father Hayes down a path and then stopped at a foundation of stone. Father bent his head and stepped through a low, narrow opening. Inside the walled space, I could see water flowing into a natural basin from an opening in the far wall. "Once a year when we were growing up," Father said, "the family would come here, and my father would dunk our heads in the water and say a prayer." He moved toward the water, leaned over, and drank from the flowing stream. Each of us stepped forward in silence to drink the water blessed by St. Moling in the year 696.

Deeper and deeper into the heart of Ireland we drove, following Father Hayes' car along what seemed to be narrower and narrower roads. At one point he pulled over and got out. "The most beautiful view in Ireland," he said, his left arm extending outward. "My mother came from the mountain in the mist; my father" — his right arm now extending in the other direction— "from that valley in the distance."

Finally, we turned up a cement-covered driveway and arrived at a farmhouse, the home of Father Hayes. Entering the living room, we were met by his mother and her warm hugs. I was instantly reminded of the Irish home I grew up in. Knick-knacks and mementos of all sorts on the tables and mantel, vases of dried flowers, paintings and family pictures on the wall, especially of a young priest newly ordained.

Having also met Essie, Jim's sister, and Mick, his brother, whose handshake was like a steel grip, we settled in for Mass. Father prayed for the Ireland that had kept the faith alive, for an end to the violence in Northern Ireland, for his deceased father, and for their guests and their safe journey in Ireland. In his reflection, he recalled how much his parents years earlier had appreciated the invitation of my wife's parents to spend some time at Raquette Lake in the Adirondacks. Mrs. Hayes eyes lit up, and she smiled. I wiped my eyes, and Essie handed Mick a tissue.

Because Brother Joe had wanted to see a calf, Mick drove us up to the back field, parked the car, and led us into an area that held about 50 head of cattle. Among the cattle there were a few calves and Fred, the bull. My childhood — a flashback. Filled with fear, my brother and I would race past the neighbor's field with the chained bull. We were both convinced that with a mere twist of his head he could break the chain that held him.

"Is Fred okay?" I asked Mick.

"Oh, he gets a bit ornery at times," Mick said, stepping over a major cow flop.

"What happens if he makes a move toward us?" Brother Joe asked.

"Run like hell for the fence and get over it before he reaches you," Mick replied.

Brother Joe did not seem thrilled at that answer, but thank God, Fred stayed relatively calm.

And then we were back at the house for dinner: chicken breasts, a huge dish of mashed potatoes, plates of carrots and peas, and slices of brown bread. We concluded with the heavenly touch of apple pie topped with a scoop of vanilla ice cream. When, with dessert completed, Essie said, "Trifle, anyone?" I could almost hear my mother's words, "Jello, anyone?"

The evening culminated perfectly when Father Hayes took us to the horse races. The racetrack reminded me of country fairs my father had taken us to when we were young, aromas of baked foods, sweet candies, fresh fruit — and then the strong scent of horses, all complemented by the easy flow of conversation that comes from people feeling at home in their world.

I did not do well until the last race, when Brother Kevin and I both bet on a horse at 8-1. The horses run clockwise in Ireland, and at this particular track, the horses actually disappeared on the far side of the track for fifty yards or so. I remember that as the horses approached the space where the track dips out of sight, my horse was near the back of the pack, but when they emerged, miracle of miracles, my horse was taking the lead. And it held the lead for the victory. With five pounds down on the horse, I ended my evening with 40 pounds.

As we said good-bye that night and headed back to Waterford, I thought of my parents journeying back to their roots, and I thought of the word *home* and how much the meaning of that word is captured in the simple acts of hospitality and generosity. The Christian Brothers at Mt. Sion in Waterford and Father Hayes and his family deep in the heart of Ireland had welcomed us home and showed us this truth.

Untranslatable

Chad, my niece's husband, had said to me, "Don't worry too much about the language. I speak very little, but I smile and wave and get pretty much what I want." Still, I carried my Spanish emergency sentences in my wallet: phonetically pronounced Spanish for "I don't speak Spanish," "I don't understand," "Where is the bathroom?" "I'm sorry," and just in case — "Help."

For a number of years, my niece Carolyn had taught Spanish literature and culture in Spain as part of her college's international study program. When she would say to me that I should come over and visit her, I would smile and say maybe someday. Not only did I not know any Spanish, I had also developed over the years a fear of flying. Then the opportunity presented itself. The chair of our high school Spanish department began in the early fall to organize a student trip to Spain for the coming spring. She asked me if I would like to chaperone, and I thought of my niece and her many requests. I said yes. Knowing the great pride each member of our Spanish department takes in the culture and language of Spain, I made a small effort to learn a little of the language — one of the zealous teachers gave me a few phrases to learn each day, but after a few weeks I put the language on the back burner and went about my teaching of English.

Having relegated the thoughts about terrorists to the far recesses of my mind, I actually found the plane flight from Newark to Madrid relaxing, chatting with students and listening to Juanes, a Columbian singer, popular in Spain and around the world. I didn't understand the words, but I liked the sound of his voice and the beat of the music.

And so we landed in Madrid, navigated through security and were on our way. Our first destination was Toledo by bus. Our driver, David, spoke very little English, so I was limited in my front-seat position to the word "gracias," whenever he would extend himself in some way to us. Arriving in Toledo, we took care of the hotel arrangements and then set out to tour the city. We walked the hilly streets of historic Toledo and listened to our guide Victor as he discussed the pervasive presence of El Greco and gave us a sense of the rich political and religious history of the city. Having toured the Catholic Cathedral and then dined in a plaza, I was feeling a bit weary and found that Linda, another teacher, and Mark, one of our students, wanted to walk back to the hotel and rest, especially since the hotel seemed only a hop, skip, and a jump away. Since the Cathedral was near the top of the city and our hotel was at the bottom, it seemed logical, as Linda said, "to just keep walking down the hill." The narrow streets did keep taking us downward, but they were bending and twisting more than we realized. When we reached the bottom of the hill, we recognized nothing. When we held our map out to a passing city dweller, she pointed out most graciously that we were on the far side of the hill, the opposite position from where we wanted to be. The map told us that it would be a long walk. We conveyed to the lady that we needed a taxi, and she called one, waiting with us and telling the driver where we needed to go. We realized how easy it was to get disoriented.

From Toledo to Cordoba and its Cathedral and historic Mosque and on to Granada, and the most stunning site of all, the Alhambra, with the magical stories of the Sultan and his selection of a "Queen for a Day." One of our female students audaciously asked the guide: "What if one of the young women did not wish to dive for the Sultan's apple?" The guide cooly responded, "Women did not think that way then."

Olive orchards as far as the eye could see dominated the landscape on our long ride north to Madrid, oceans of olive trees. In Madrid, we settled into the most elegant hotel of the trip, and there I made a call to my niece. My chaperone duties had been suspended for the evening so that I could enjoy dinner with her and her family. Chad was at home, and he gave me directions. "Because the apartment complex is tricky to find," — he explained how to find it — "it is better to have the taxi driver drop you off at the intersection of Reina Cristina and Andrés Torrejón."

I had written down the street names and then asked one of the Spanish teachers to pronounce the two names for me. I practiced a few times in her presence, and then I was off, flagging down a taxi in front of the hotel. I had a laugh just as I was about to get into the taxi when Robert, one of our students, responded to my question about what he and his crew were doing for dinner with, "Going out for tapas." I said, "Great — where are you going?" And he said, "Burger King." I retorted, "Tapas at Burger King?" And he smiled and said, "French Fries."

The driver stared at my paper with the street names on it — I also had written the Spanish word for intersection before the names. He stared and we were off.

Watching the meter continue to ring up euros while we sat still in a tunnel was my first signal that trouble was brewing. In the back of the taxi, I began muttering my frustration — "I don't think this is right." Chad had said that the trip would take about twenty minutes, and we were close to forty at that point. Finally emerging from the tunnel, my driver swung onto an expressway, and we began moving at a good clip, seemingly away from the city. My tipping point came as we passed two signs, one for the airport and one for Barcelona. My piece of paper had become part of an ancient popcorn-making machine — I kept flipping it rapidly in the air. I probably should have yelled out the only word in my lexicon that made any sense in the context — "Ayuda!" — help! But I did the only thing a desperate man with no language skills in a foreign country could do — I leaned up over the seat with the piece of paper in my hand and said, "No!" He pointed at the paper and said, "Sí!" I returned a louder "No" and made a crossing gesture with my hands and then pointed to the center of the two street names.

For a moment the only response was more speed; now that I think of it, he was probably as frustrated as I was for he knew, all evidence indicated, no English. He also knew that he had one angry passenger.

Suddenly he turned and we shot down an exit ramp. I was fairly sure that he would stop the car, get out and come around to open my door, and signal me to get out. But he didn't — he made a u-turn, and drove back up the opposite ramp and we were heading back to the city. Now he was speaking a number of Spanish words, which were, I am sure, an indication of his own exasperation. Yes, we were kindred spirits.

We still had a moment of truth ahead. When we stopped at the intersection of the two streets, his meter read 38.50 euros, by the exchange rate more than fifty dollars. I handed him a twenty euro bill, said, "That's all I'm paying," and got out of his car. He burst out with a profusion of Spanish expletives and then sped off.

Chad greeted me at the door with a smile of relief and the words, "We're so sorry. We called the hotel when we didn't hear from you. We knew something must have happened. Carolyn ran down to the corner store to get a couple of items — she'll be right back, but come to the balcony and let me show you something." We walked out onto the balcony that overlooked the city, and Chad said, "See that tower over there" — he pointed to the left, and I saw it, perhaps a half mile away — "your hotel is right next to it."

After their four children were put to bed, Chad, Carolyn, their good friend Carlos, a writer, and I sat at their kitchen table, drinking wine, enjoying some good cheeses, and some amazing olives. Carolyn explained that there had been an American military base in the town Andrés Torrejón outside the city, but it had closed. Perhaps that might have been the reason for the driver's confusion.

As evening settled over Madrid and the city became a constellation of lights, it came to me that the warm conversation of good friends and the taste of wine and olives were two things that make Spain so special.

Later that night, Carolyn and I walked back to the hotel. When she got a taxi back from the hotel, she told me the meter read 4.80 euros.

The O'Brien Family: On the left, I am in the arms of my brother Leo. Next to Leo is my mother, Anna. To the right of her is Rose, my sister, and then Harold, my father, holds my brother John.

My first day of school. Leo stands with his foot on the running board, and John peeks out from behind his left arm.

Our home in Raymertown, in and around which so many of our childhood adventures took place. (A watercolor painted by my brother-in-law, Hank Damm).

123

Camp Tekakwitha, Lake Luzerne. I am number 99.

Our foursome at Seaview Golf Resort: from the left — John, Colin, Leo, and Paul

St. Moling's Well, St. Mullins, Ireland. This well was blessed by St. Moling in 696. We drank from it and blessed ourselves with its water.

CT, our cat.

North Point, Raquette Lake.

The Best-Laid Plans

It had been a long November week in the classroom, and the weekend looked better than ever. The key would be Saturday's football game against Christian Brothers Academy, a perennial powerhouse and a big favorite, but with Chris Haggerty at quarterback and John Nealon anchoring our defense, we had a shot, and if it helped, the home field advantage.

The phone rang Friday afternoon shortly after I got to my apartment. "Hey, Paul — going ok?" My father was on the line — always a minimalist in phone conversations.

"Long week, Dad, but happy it's Friday."

A pause, "Listen, I need a little help tomorrow."

I waited. "Sure, what's up?"

"Doctor says I've got to get this test — and he scheduled me tomorrow morning at 10 at the Leonard."

"Should be no problem," I said, my mind quickly calculating that I would have plenty of time to get to the 1 p.m. start of the game. "I will see you about 9:15 tomorrow."

'See ya then," he said and was gone.

It was roughly 10:50 when my father appeared in the hospital waiting room after his test. He was moving slowly, and I kind of walked along side of him to the car.

"Let's go down to Cappy's," he said.

"What's that?" I asked.

"A little grill on River Street."

I glanced at my watch, still time to catch the one o'clock start of the game.

As we entered the bar, I felt that I was accompanying a celebrity. Cries of "Red" (my father's old nickname because he had been a redhead), "Harold," "Heh, Buddy," — a chorus of hellos from the bartender and five or so customers, all about my father's age. I felt as if I had stumbled into a secret club.

"Dave, this is my son Paul — he's a teacher," my father said as we sat down at two stools. Dave reached out to me, "Good meeting ya, son. What can I get ya? Got your Dad's boilermaker ready to go."

"I'll just have a draft beer," I said, as I watched Dave place a shot of whiskey in front of my father. He then drew two glasses of beer and placed one in front of me and one in front of Dad. He had a half glass of something dark near the cash register and picked it up. "Paul," he said, "I just want to make a toast to your Dad. Guys," — he turned and looked at the two guys to his left and then back at the others — "this toast is to Red, good to see you back, and we wish you all the best." The others joined in lifting their classes and looking at my Dad, who sat quietly, head down a bit but with a little smile.

Although it was early in the day for me to drink beer, I finished my glass, and Dave filled it immediately. I knew I needed to nurse the second, as we sat chatting with Dave about Troy politics, football, and old friends they both knew — mostly Dave talking and my father nodding and smiling. After about an hour, my father tapped me on the shoulder and said, "Better get going." He started to reach for his wallet, but Dave said, "Harold, got ya covered. You're the best ." And then Dave reached out to me and shook my hand, "Good to meet a son of Harold's," he said. As we started to leave, Dave and I shared a look of concern and then Dave reached to remove Dad's drink glasses, still almost full.

Outside, I started the car and thought that I still had time to make the game. And then my father's words, "Let's go down to the El Dorado."

"Really," I said.

"Yeah, I got to see a few guys."

I looked at my watch and sensed that the game was getting out of reach.

I knew of the El Dorado because it was across the street from Manory's, a popular hangout when we were in high school. I even remember a few times walking in front of the El Dorado and breathing in the intoxicating aroma of beer and whiskey.

We entered to a much stronger range of greetings. I felt as if I were with a war hero. Some guys standing at the bar moved so that my father and I had seats. "Good to see ya, Red," "Great to have you back, Red," and a variety of welcomes, with pats on the back to go along.

"Mickey, this is my son, the teacher," and we were off again to a draft for me, a boilermaker for my father, and then the conversation, but this time interrupted often by people coming up, touching my father, slapping him on the back, and offering tidbits from their lives. I knew it was coming. Mickey picked up what looked like a beer, "Hey, everyone," he shouted, "want to salute Red, glad he's here with us, and tell you what, guys, this place will always be a home for Red."

It was closing in on 2 o'clock when we left; the game had been eclipsed by my father's world and his friends. I had had another beer and a half and yes, my father barely touched his boilermaker, but I now knew that something else was going on. He was sharing a part of his life that mattered with me. That day was the last time he appeared at those taverns and the last time we shared so much together.

Good-bye, Lash LaRue

I started buying comic books when I was eight years old. I liked the bright drawings, the dramatic figures, and the clear narrative line. On one occasion when my parents, my younger brother, and I were starting out on a trip to Baltimore to visit my older bother who was studying for the priesthood, my mother handed me a dollar and said, "This is your spending money for the trip." I knew what that dollar would buy.

When we stopped at a drugstore luncheonette for something to eat, I immediately spotted a magazine stand. The comic book section looked enormous. I raced through my tuna sandwich, gulped down my milk, and then asked my parents if I could walk around the drugstore.

What a selection! So many to choose from. And what made the experience so precious was the fact that the comic books were only ten cents each. Lash Larue, Batman, Superman, Roy Rogers, Archie and on and on. I had found gold. In a few minutes, I possessed ten.

Returning to the table holding the bag with my comic books, I could barely contain my desire to be back on the road so that I could begin to read. My mother looked at the bag. "Did you spend your dollar already?" she asked. "Yes," I said, and held out the open bag so that she could see. She frowned, "You spent your entire dollar on those?" I nodded, and she said, "I don't want you spending all your money on comic books — it's foolish." I said, "Ok, Mom," but the thought that ran through my mind as we headed toward the car was that when I got older and made my own money, I would buy as many comics as I wanted. I would fill my huge old Victorian house with stacks and stacks and stacks of comic books.

By the time I was a teenager, my love of comic books had been replaced by sports' magazines, entertainment magazines with stories about Ricky Nelson, Troy Donahue, and other heroes, and even adult magazines like *Real Men* and *True Detective*.

My real love for books did not bloom until college. I remember as a freshman my roommate staring in disbelief as I held his copy of *The Catcher in the Rye*, " I can't believe you haven't read it," he said. The allusions to books never read, bibliographies of long lists of books given out in class, discussions at the College Diner and the Beechmont of books that seemed compelling and beguiling — and that growing realization, never too late, of all the fantastic and mysterious and richly complex worlds waiting for my mind to find them. Thus bookstores became my oasis in every city I visited.

The Mistletoe Bookstore in Albany was the first bookstore that seemed to offer so much more than best sellers. It had two levels of books and a wonderful selection of a world I was just discovering — literary essays, biographies, criticism. I remember once buying almost all of my Christmas presents at the Mistletoe. The Saville Bookstore in Washington, D.C. was for me what the baseball field in Iowa was for Shoeless Joe Jackson. A colonial house transformed into a book store. You could wander from room to room and become weak with the possibilities. I found the equivalent years later in the Hathaway Bookstore in Wellesley, MA. In both bookstores, I felt the euphoria I had experienced in front of the comic books in the drugstore years ago.

Once college and grad school were over and I had started to teach, my search continued. While some people went to New York for theater or for shopping or for the beat of the City, I went in search of bookstores. Three Lives and Company, the Strand, Scribner's — I loved the look and feel of the store — and the Gotham Bookmark are a few that stand out in my mind. I remember how excited I was when the gnome emerged from an underground room at the Gotham Bookmark holding in his hand the book I had searched for, *The Mind-Reader*, a collection of poems by Richard Wilbur.

Having married a woman who is a major reader and loves bookstores certainly brightened the journey. To Saratoga and the Montana Bookstore, which was with its book-lined walls, hanging plants, and comfortable chairs like someone's personal library. To vacation sites and visits to towns and cities of friends where we would always inquire at some point about the local bookstores. Like the Kennebunk Book Port on the coast of Maine, the Concord Bookshop in Concord, MA, the Andover Bookstore in Andover, MA, a Bunch of Grapes on Martha's Vineyard, and Chapter Two in Charleston, South Carolina. I remember visiting my sister-in-law for a few sweltering days in Charleston, and the coolest oasis I found in town was the bookstore.

For a period of time, my wife and I would sojourn over to Amherst and South Hadley, MA, to visit the many bookstores: the Albion, The Jeffrey Amherst and the Odyssey Book Shop among our favorites. The Odyssey with its gentle and gracious proprietor, Romeo Grenier, moved for some time to the top of my list of favorite bookstores. I loved its range of books, the design of the shop, and its warm and welcoming atmosphere; of course, it had the advantage of its name, echoing Homer's great epic.

Over the years, the book world has changed, influenced to some degree by the rise of technology, the competition of the visual arts, and the many lures of our modern world, often to the detriment of time spent in the world of reading. I have witnessed the closing of many of my favorite bookstores, including Scribners, The Gotham Bookmart, and Chapter Two. The arrival of the Big Bookstores like Borders and Barnes and Noble filled the vacuum for a period of time, though rarely having the appeal of the small store. Borders, on Wolf Road in Albany, was the one exception — a large bookstore that had the feel of a much smaller book store, with a welcoming ambience that made you want to read. I can't recount the number of times my wife and I would go to the Wolf Road Borders after dinner or for something to do on a weekend night. You could find an easy chair in many places or a table in the coffee shop and just get lost in the books. Sadly, that store closed.

Three bookstores in the immediate area still glow in this modern mercantile world: The Open Door in downtown Schenectady; The Book House in Stuyvesant Plaza, Albany, which also features a major children's section; and in Saratoga, there is the excellent Northshire Bookstore, a sister of the Manchester, Vermont store. All three still give readers hope.

I rarely ever threw a book away, maybe gave some away, but for the most part, every book that I bought and most that my wife bought are in bookcases throughout the house. No Victorian mansion, our home is a small, brick ranch. And books are everywhere. I have only a few comic books now, and those are the comic book versions of classic texts, but the dream of long ago has been fulfilled in the form of books. The space for more books is running out, and I am starting to give more books away. Not for me an easy task. For the books all have a feel and a history. All have offered their worlds. Worlds of words that have made my journey so much richer.

Eastern Point

For thirty years, Eastern Point Jesuit Retreat House in Gloucester, Massachusetts, has been a key for Debbie and me, a place to be at peace and experience the beauty of silence.

We had heard of the Silent Retreat Weekends at Eastern Point from my sister and brother-in-law, who had started making the retreats there in the late 70's. They had spoken of the Jesuit retreat leaders, the power of silence, and the beautiful setting on the Atlantic coast. And so with their strong recommendation, my wife and I decided to make a Silent Retreat Weekend.

We had not planned on the Route 128 traffic north, and it looked doubtful that we would make the Friday night dinner. We had also not anticipated the trickiness of the directions, especially in the dark and the rain. We found E. Main Street, which dissolved into Eastern Point Road and then Eastern Point Boulevard, but in the dark tight roads, we missed a small sign for the retreat house and Toronto Avenue, ending up on Fort Hill Ave. Realizing our mistake, we turned around and found Toronto, which led to Niles Pond Road. We could have been anywhere, a narrow road between two encroaching thickets of brush. And then we spotted a small sign with an arrow to the right — Retreat House.

No one could have made us feel more welcome than Sister Dorothy, a member of the retreat team. She had us sign in and then explained where we were staying and the time of the first gathering. She also said that there was some food left. I chose to have some of the baked cod, and Debbie went off to her room to get settled. As I was leaving the large dining room that looked out at the Atlantic Ocean, Sister Dorothy stopped me and said, "As you know each person has his own room, and your wife's is on the second floor of the wing, and you are on the first, but if you want to pop up there to say hello now, that's ok." I smiled, checked our room numbers again, and was off.

To get to the wing, you had to pass through a long unheated walkway, and as I made my way along it, I could hear the wind howling and the freezing rain against the windows. In my room on the first floor, I looked out into the night. I knew that the ocean was out there, and that was pretty exciting. I adjusted the radiator heat controls and then made the bed with the clean sheets and pillow cases that had been left. A desk, a *Bible*, a narrow coat rack. What more could I want? I checked my watch and observed that I had twenty minutes until the first session.

As I sat in the gathering room next to Debbie listening to each of the sixty or so other retreatants, I was overwhelmed by their stories. Each of us had been asked to say briefly who we were and why we were there. So many stories: From having cared over the last year for a dying parent ... to raising five children and never having time for oneself ... to winning a battle against alcoholism and now needing time with the Lord. The whole room seemed permeated with spiritual longing. Then Sister Dorothy told us that what each person looked forward to most of all on this weekend was silence, and from this moment on, silence was to be respected.

Images that remain fixed in my mind — perhaps shaped by later visits to Eastern Point once or twice a year over the next thirty years: the red pulsing beam of the lighthouse from the dining room late at night; two swans in stillness on the far side of Niles Pond; the fireplace room with its dark wood paneling, and shadows on the wall from the flickering fire; the thick brush along the narrow path down to the ocean; the clean, simple rooms. What Eastern Point offered came close to what Thoreau said was his reason for going to the woods " — to front the essential facts of life."

Keys on the Road

For me, time opened up, expanded, gave me that feeling I have when I am with people who allow you to be yourself. I especially loved the time between the optional talks, talks that concluded with suggested spiritual passages, when I could take a walk or curl up for a nap. And silence was golden to all: people gave full respect to the retreat's expectation of silence so that each person could be free of the mundane interruptions and messages of everyday life in order to focus on one's own spiritual needs. At dinner, with classical music playing, the only other sound was the clicking of cutlery on plates or a dish being put into the to-be-cleaned bin. I loved the nights too — late into the night, heading down to the dining room, pouring a coffee or tea and reading or watching the recurring pattern of the ocean waves, reflected in the moonlight or the offshore lights. If you met someone, you passed silently as companions on a road, sometimes giving a slight recognition as if to say, "Isn't this great?" And "Don't you love silence?"

But occasionally there were the stories that you could not ignore, stories that were part of your day. I think it was the third year we attended a weekend, and once again it was a cold, rainy weekend. Being back at Eastern Point, however, always heightened the experience of living. It was just good to be back again.

I heard the chronic, dry, rasping cough from the person in the next room long before I went to bed. It was one of those coughs that leave you kind of helpless as you try to fend it off — your body is dealing with something you can't control. I lay down in my bed and realized that his bed was placed on the right side of the room, mine the left, and he was only a few inches away. I turned away from the wall, but the cough kept coming — sometimes for long stretches that ended in a kind of wheezing, whimpering cry. When he stopped, the counterpoint was the wind and the rain against the window. I think I drifted off finally and woke to silence. When I left my room to head for the community bathroom and shower, I passed his room, door slightly ajar, but he was not there. Over the next day and into the evening, I did not see the person go in or out of his room. And at our meetings, I scanned the 60 or so people to see if I could figure out who it was, but since we were divided into two groups and faced each other, there were often two or three rows behind me. I had arrived at three possibilities, but I just couldn't be sure. The second night the cough started again — and it continued. A long battle into the night. I turned away and tried to sleep, I sat up to try to read, I dressed and walked to the dining room — I imagined he might have heard me get up and might join me, but he didn't. That morning I met him.

It was early and though I was tired, I wanted to walk down to the ocean and see the morning sunrise, especially after the coastal storm of the two previous days. When you are on a retreat, nature can take on special power, not always present in your standard sunrises and sunsets. As I left my room, I noticed that his door was ajar — maybe he was seeking relief for his cough somewhere. I walked down to the far end of our dorm and headed out the door toward the ocean. On a lone white bench facing the ocean sat a hooded person. The path down to the ocean was at a nearly right angle to the bench, about fifty or so feet away. I turned and walked down the path — part wood, part rock — to the ocean. The waves were exploding with light as they pounded the huge rocks. I climbed over a series of smaller rocks until I reached some the size of mansions. Standing on one rock, I glanced around — I was alone. For a minute I thought of Stephen Crane's poem, "A Man Said to the Universe," but chose not to align my mind with the resolution of that little dramatic poem. Instead my mind turned to Eliot's "Dry Salvages," and I reflected on how the patterns of one's past when merged with the experience of the spiritual, here in the sun dancing on the rushing water, can bring a redeeming coherence to one's life. And then I thought of the Greek hero Hector — we had just finished *The Iliad* in AP English — and how noble and courageous he was, especially at the moment he faced the awful reality of Achilles. He knows he cannot defeat Achilles, and yet he is willing to do all he can to defend the City of Troy. Time had collapsed. I was alone. More crashing waves. Then glancing at my watch, I realized that I needed to get moving if I wanted to make breakfast.

Just as I reached the top of the pathway, the figure on the bench turned towards me. The light from the sun seemed to reach in and touch his eyes, eyes deep inside the hood. He looked spectral and his whole body appeared emaciated. Maybe the look was for three seconds at the most, and then he turned back towards the sea. I walked on. So many thoughts raced through my mind, but what dominated was that this man faced death and that this weekend was probably one in which he was trying to come to terms with that reality. When I got back to my room, I sat down at the desk and wrote this poem:

Eastern Point

He sat on the lone white bench
Staring out to sea where
Wind-swept waves crested
Into mythological creatures.

Hood up and hands buried
Deep within, he seemed to be
One who had heard
A dark message

It was a cold December morning
Though the sun was finally emerging
The cold of the coastal storm
Would, I was sure, cling tenaciously.

I had continued past the specter
On a slippery, planked path

That twisted and turned through thick brambles
Down to the irrepressible waters
Cutting and sliding
On sudden surges of air
Gulls screamed out their songs
Above the charged and churning sea.

I was lost in time
Outside the walled city of Troy
Where the battle raged —
Shoulder to shoulder I stood with Hector

Waiting, waiting, waiting
For the inexorable onslaught
Together we held
The thinnest thread of hope

On my return I could see
That he had not budged
But as I neared
He turned slowly towards me.

His black protruding eyes
Caught the fire of the rising sun
Then they withdrew into the hooded shadow
Of his ashen and emaciated face.

Glancing back from the lawn above
I could see the hooded figure
Once again looking seaward
Waiting, waiting, waiting.

Raquette Lake

My wife used to say that Buddy's (her father) Church was Raquette Lake, that there was nothing that came closer to a spiritual force for him than when he was sitting out on the lake in the early morning with the line of his fishing pole in the water. It didn't really matter if he caught anything; just being there was everything. My first visit to Raquette was in 1971 with my brother, and I still remember the eleven mile road in from Route 28 — would it go on forever? Since that time I have come to sense that the road is the marker that you have arrived; I have also come to sense what the lake meant to Buddy. I close the book with two stories about Raquette, the first a reflection on what the lake meant to him.

I am alone. Floating in a styrofoam supported lounge chair about fifty yards from shore. About a half-hour earlier, the *W. W. Durant (*a boat named after William West Durant, the great designer and developer of camps in the Adirondacks*)* on its dinner cruise passed by the bay where the family house is. Shortly after the Durant disappeared around the bend, Debbie, who is part fish, urged me to jump into the water because the water was so "refreshing."

And so I did, doing a back flip onto the floating chair. She was right. Warmed by three hot days, the water was perfect, silky and smooth, without any of the biting cold currents I have known at Raquette Lake.

I paddle with my hands past the neighbor's boathouse and around the bend to look at the new house that our neighbor, a man of some means, is building for himself and his family, a kind of Kennedy-like compound. As I gaze at his smaller house on the point and then at the main house, I see his architectural design and its aesthetics. The houses, almost golden brown, have been done in a style that respects the natural world. He hasn't blasted everything away in the front of his house to scream, "Look at me!"

The water is so calm. I lean back in the chair and close my eyes. In the gentlest way, the water, like a caring mother, rocks the chair. It is difficult to say how comfortable I feel at this moment, maybe the way you feel in bed on a chilly night after you and the bed have created the ideal cozy space. In this early evening stillness, the water laps the chair. The only other sounds I hear now are the distant churning of the Durant's engine and the faint voices of campers from Quaker Beach across the waters.

That morning I was propped up in bed reading David Baldacci's novel *Wish You Well,* the story of a young woman who returns to her father's Virginia home after he has been killed in a car accident. It is in living with her grandmother in this home that she begins to understand the forces that shaped her father into the writer he became. As I read, I could hear a faint conversation from downstairs and a low but pretty constant whistling of an unrecognizable tune, sort of a counterpoint to the talk.

Debbie enters the bedroom bringing with her the aromas of coffee and bacon. "I need your help," she says.

"Sure," I respond, thinking she wants me to help with the breakfast, probably to cut fruit.

"Take Buddy out on his boat. I can't make breakfast and do that too."

"Deb, I've never driven a boat, let alone his boat."

"Please, just do it. He needs to get out there. Don't worry, it's like driving a car."

She is serious. "Ok," I said, "but he has to back the boat out."

I knew that Buddy had always found the early morning solo cruise a prayerful and rejuvenating experience. Often he would take his fishing pole along, but the few times he caught a fish, he would throw it back in. During the past year, substantial health problems had severely limited much of what he loved to do, including his morning boat rides alone on the lake.

He is pacing on the deck when I step outside. "I'll take a shot at driving your boat if you want to go out on the lake," I say. With his jacket and fishing hat on, he is already moving toward the stairs and responds, "Sounds good."

On the dock, I say to him, "You back it out, and when you get the boat turned around, I can take over."

"Fine," he says.

Once seated, he turns the key of the fourteen-foot boat powered by a 120 horsepower motor, and the boat throbs with life. Backing it out effortlessly, he makes a slow sweeping turn and faces the lake. I want him to stay at the controls, but he knows the rules he now lives by, and we awkwardly change seats.

"Throttle forward," he says, and I begin to slowly ease the handle forward. The boat seems uncertain with its new captain.

"Push it forward," he says, gesturing with a strong forward motion. I follow his direction, and the boat leaps upward, leaving me for a second staring at the blue sky. And then the boat comes back down, and we are sailing across the waters with the lake and the mountains now opening up in front of us.

"You have to go up first in order to get back to a level plane," he says, and I think of how different this advice is from Virgil's advice to Dante as they prepare to visit the Inferno.

I have settled in somewhat and am actually enjoying the ride. Except for one boat, crossing our path in the distance, we are alone out here. He gives me a few tips about when to ease up, how far to keep from the buoys, and how to cross a wake, but most of the time he seems to be simply enjoying the lake and the world he has known for forty years. A world he brought his wife and family of seven to, at first renting a house, and then buying property and having his own house built in a small cove in North Bay. He kept a close eye on the building of that house, visiting the lake as often as he could until it was done. Medicine had been his calling, and through hard work he had built a good practice in Schenectady. Then he made a transition to hospital administration, committing himself fully to that job, until his own failing health told him it was time to step down. Not easy for a strong, independent spirit, but it was time. And always, it seemed, there had been the lake to lift him up and give balance and peace to his life.

"Better head back," he says, and I turn the boat in the direction of North Point. As we approach the cove, I can feel some tension building about docking the boat. This time we can't bend the rules and switch positions. The dock comes at me too quickly, and then his voice, "Turn the wheel right, that's it, nice and easy, a little slower." And then Debbie is walking down the dock and sees that the front of the boat has drifted a little wide. She reaches out for the boat, and with her hand eases us in. Secure, I stand and step back as he steps on the driver's seat and then, reaching for Debbie's hand, onto the dock. He turns back to me, "Thank you."

Nearly dusk out on the lake now, and in my floating chair, I hear the fading cry of the Durant engine. I look across the lake. There is not a soul in sight. My hands slip into the water. As I ease along, I sense more than ever the healing power of water.

Ending and Beginning

Glancing at the speedometer, I see that I am cruising at 24 miles an hour. My right arm is almost numb from the weight of the book, so I shift it to my left. Looking out through the open venetian blinds, I see that it is still raining, but it's more like a heavy mist. Raquette Lake appears relatively calm, but the dock and the boat are not offering an invitation today, nor have they for the last day and a half. In one sense, I am thrilled for I have read over 400 pages of *The Order of the Phoenix* since we arrived on Sunday night, much of it on the stationary bike located in front of the basement window that looks out on the lake. There is something about pedaling along on the bicycle that is congruent with my reading of the book, especially now that Harry, Ron, Hermione, Ginny, Neville, and Luna are in the midst of a battle with the Death Eaters.

I had pre-ordered the book as did many others and picked it up at the bookstore the day it arrived. On Monday following the release of the book, I was informed by one of my favorite students (a great reader) that she had purchased the book at 1:03 a.m. on Saturday — the bookstore had been open super-late to allow for the sale of the book — arrived home and read for five hours, slept for three, then finished the book in eleven more hours. About a week later, I started the book and over the next few weeks plodded along slowly, but there were so many distractions — television, computer, papers, magazines, phone chats — that I could not focus and accomplish much of anything. Even on a trip to the Cape, reading was eclipsed by frequent games of progressive rummy. Until this past Sunday afternoon.

Traveling up Route 28 through Warrensburg, North Creek, Indian Lake, and Blue Mountain, we could see the clouds concentrating and beginning to dominate the mountains we were now in. By the time we reached Raquette Lake, there was no question that the dock would not be the gathering place of choice over the coming days. Standing on the dock under dark, heavy clouds, I could see that we were alone in the Bay.

One thing about being in the family house at night is that quiet looms large; without the distraction of television and the city — no Stewart's a stone's throw away for me to run to — life becomes cleaner, simpler, more focused. After I washed the dishes on Sunday night, I descended into the basement, climbed onto the old Schwinn stationary bicycle — a great machine — and set off into Harry Potter's world. On my forty-mile journey — on a regular bike I could have ridden into Long Lake's Stewart's, had a coffee, and returned to the house — I listened to Hagrid tell his tale of meeting the Giants, experienced evil as it took a serpent's grip on Harry, visited St. Mungo's Hospital for Magical Maladies and Injuries, and spent Christmas with Harry as he struggled with the darkness within himself, despite the efforts of Hermione, Sirius, and others to lift his spirits.

And so for the next day and a half, reading dominated my life. My wife was well into *The Time of Our Singing* by Richard Powers, and she was as preoccupied as I. I read primarily on the bike, but also late at night in bed when the only other sounds were the mysterious and scary creatures that were right outside our door.

Occasionally, I would pause and think about why this book had taken such a hold of the hearts and imaginations of so many, especially the young. Many of the reviewers had spoken about the author's grasp of the emotional turmoil of adolescence and the awful pressures adolescents feel as they try to find a basic coherence in their lives. From a teacher's perspective, I could see how well Rowling grasps the old truth that what you give is what you get and that those teachers who respect Harry and his friends and give them room to be and grow are rewarded in one way or another and that those teachers who are mean-spirited and intolerant pay a price. And then I would think that when you really got down to it, the book was as translator Robert Fagles called Homer's *Odyssey* simply a "rip-roaring good yarn."

When all is said and done, people do like a good story. And look at me — I had traveled over a hundred and twenty miles on this bike reading Harry's story.

On Tuesday morning, I approached the end of *The Order of the Phoenix,* all distractions wiped away by the writing skill of J. K. Rowling and the peace and quiet of Raquette Lake.

As Harry prepares to return to Privet Drive and spend the summer with the Dursleys, he looks at his friends who have come to bid him good-bye.

"We'll see you soon, mate," says Ron, and Hermione adds, "Really soon, Harry, we promise." Harry cannot find words to tell them what their presence means; he simply smiles, waves farewell, and walks out of the station ahead of the Dursleys.

My time now with Harry is over. Harry is going back to the Dursleys. And his journey will continue. Our stay at Raquette Lake is nearly over. I will return to my world and all its distractions and duties. And my journey will continue.

Paul O'Brien taught English for forty-seven years at Notre Dame and Notre Dame-Bishop Gibbons School. Since leaving the classroom, he has remained active in a number of educational boards including the Notre Dame-Bishop Gibbons School Board, the St. Kateri Tekakwitha School Board and the New York State English Council Executive Board. His hobbies include reading, writing, traveling, and meeting good friends at the Blue Ribbon Diner for breakfast or lunch. He lives with his wife Deborah and cat CT in Niskayuna, New York.